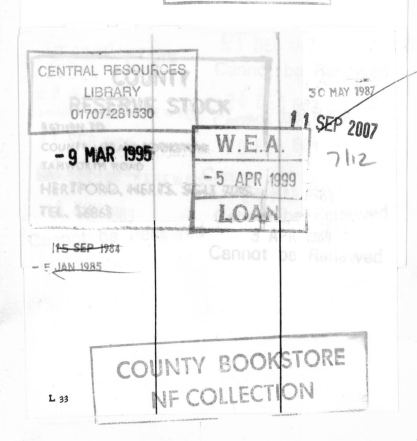

I Knew My Place

I Knew My Place

EDWARD SHORT

MACDONALD & CO
LONDON & SYDNEY

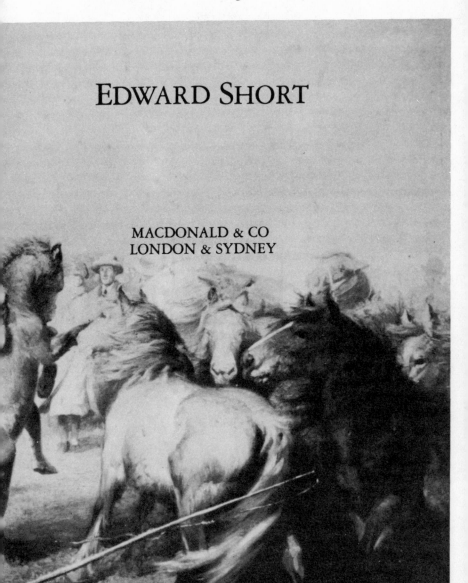

Contents

Foreword

THIS IS THE STORY of the first decade of my life – well, more or less for here and there I have strayed into the second decade when it suited me to do so.

More important, it is a portrait of the remote rural community into which I was born and in which I spent my early, formative years.

I hope it will be seen – for I certainly intend it to be – as a tribute to the gentle folks who nurtured me, who taught me, who protected me. I am what they made me, and whether they would have approved of their creation or not I owe them more than I can ever repay.

It is about a village at the watershed between centuries of seclusion and the strident new age which dawned with the First World War and of which the motor car and the wireless were the harbingers.

In an age when so much of our lives is determined by science and technology it is both pleasant and important to look back occasionally to quieter days and simpler ways.

Apart from all this, like many other people, I have never been able to get my childhood out of my system. It needs to be exorcised. The recalling and baring of it here will, I hope, quieten it. Perhaps it will now let me be.

Earliest Recollections

BETWEEN THE CRAGGY PEAKS of the Lake District and the round-topped fells of the Pennines there is a wedge of a valley, the lovely valley of the Eden. It is a country of green farms, of sombre woods and furtive streams. At the wide end are the bird-filled salt-marshes of the Solway; at the apex is the old limestone market town of Kirkby Stephen below Wild Boar Fell.

In times past the valley was the major route between the border fortress of Carlisle and the great northern capital of York. The Roman road, straight as a die, runs through it and is for long stretches the A66. Medieval kings passed along it on their journeys around their kingdom – Malleus Scotorum most of all. They built a string of castles along it at Carlisle, Penrith, Brougham, Appleby, Warcop – demolished in 1606 for building stone – and Brough.

It was in the remote village of Warcop that I was born of parents whose roots run back through the centuries in many parish registers in what was then the neighbouring county of Cumberland.

Everywhere in the area there are signs of early man, a hill settlement with the rectangular huts of its ancient occupants still clearly etched in the grass, a moated fort in the glebe field adjoining the churchyard, stone circles and many tumuli. Warcop was old when the Romans drove their road through the valley and very old when the medieval kings built their castles along it. I suppose it developed where it did because of its fertile soil, its excellent supply of crystal clear water from the limestone fells and its surrounding shelter of low hills as well, of course, as the fells themselves which enclosed the valley. It was twice blessed, a sheltered site in a sheltered valley.

The nearest towns are Carlisle and Darlington, thirty-six and forty miles away respectively. This isolation gave it a remarkable continuity both physically and socially. The same family names crop up over long periods of its history. The Warcop family itself persisted in the parish from the thirteenth to the end of the sixteenth century. Many of the family names recorded in the 1829 edition of the Directory of Cumberland and Westmorland were still there in 1929. But the persistent names were in the main the families who worked on the land and not the gentry (a word we generally used – with 'toffs' or 'nobs' as alternatives). Indeed they were the incomers, only having lived there for two or three generations though they would have hated to be reminded of this.

Place names in the parish, the names of fields, hills, gills, streams etc, are of great antiquity, e.g. the high land to the south of the village where I spent countless carefree days in my childhood was known as Hubers. It appears in an agreement made in Latin between the monks of Byland Abbey and certain local gentlemen in 1194 as Hobergha. The farm, Ploughlands, was Plowland in at least four of the Byland charters in the twelfth, thirteenth and fourteenth centuries. Fouldberhill was first mentioned as Faldebergha in 1158.

The continuity in the shape and look of the village was, as far as one could tell, no less remarkable. Divided both physically and psychologically by the beck, it was tadpole-shaped with a clumpy head and straggling tail which petered out a few hundred yards to the south-west.

Its nucleus, including the grandly named 'The Square', as well as two shops, the Post Office, one inn, the Reading Room, station, school, church, smithy, one farm and most of the gentry houses, was 'ower t'beck'. This was, as you would expect, the Church/Tory side of the village. The other half, the straggling tail where we lived, had two shops, one inn, two chapels, the Temperance Hall and Temperance Institute, the sawmill, a number of farms and one 'big' house where a

11

newcomer lived who was not really counted among the elect. Our side was the Liberal/Non-conformist half. There were, of course, exceptions to this grouping on both sides of the beck, but broadly it was a political denominational division and, the 'ower t'beck' people believed, a social one as well, for they fancied themselves because of their closer proximity to the village establishment.

Up to the middle twenties, when four new houses were built, no-one could remember when the last house had been built from scratch. Some had been altered out of all recognition, over the years, like The Tower, a farmhouse which had been the original manor house, or the Mill House, a minor gentry house which I remember being created from the miller's small cottage, or, indeed, our own house which before the turn of the century had been a farm building. In many houses there were signs of long forgotten alterations such as blocked up windows and doors; in some cases the outline of the broad doors of a barn remained in a cottage wall. They had all the marks, and the feel, of having been lived in for a long, long time.

I always thought the houses resembled the people. Apart from a short row of mid-nineteenth century two-up, two-down cottages, they looked like a haphazard crowd of old, rather squat, strong men, each one different, each one holding his ground against all comers.

The biggest and most interesting house was The Hall, the residence – indeed The Residence – of the Lady of the Manor, (her husband died in 1922). It was interesting partly, I think, because it was the major repository of influence and power in the village but also because the Elizabethan and Georgian parts of it were to be seen clearly on the front elevation. The interior, and it was a rare event for any of us to be allowed inside, was equally clearly demarcated with a Tudor great hall at one side, a quite beautiful Georgian room in the centre leading into a large panelled library on the other side. But more of The Hall and its occupant later.

The old sandstone church in which I was christened and confirmed was dedicated to the Ionian missionary, St Columba. It was the oldest building in the parish but was not in any way architecturally remarkable; like the rest of the village it was squat and strong, the product of centuries of building, of additions and alterations. The lower wall of the nave was probably part of a twelfth century church. The two transepts and the chancel arch were added in the thirteenth century and the south aisle two hundred years later. It was lighted by inefficient and very smelly gas lighting. The gas was produced by chemicals in a contraption with long chains and pulleys worked by the vicar.

The porch dated from the sixteenth century and, as it had no door, it was, together with the seats in the oak lych gate, a favourite resort of couples on wet nights. I hope the ancient builders would have approved the profane use to which later generations put their work. The lych gate had been built to commemorate a member of the manorial family killed in the Crimea.

The Lady of the Manor claimed that she owned the chancel because, as so often occurred, there was a Victorian re-building largely paid for by one of her predecessors. Fortunately it was limited to the chancel, unlike many other parishes where beautiful medieval churches were destroyed because of the nineteenth century passion for 'improvement'. Maybe the Lord of the Manor at the time was hard up – or mean, but whatever the reason, the church escaped modernization and remained as a monument to many generations of Warcop people.

In 1862 gangs of Irish labourers built the single track railway along the valley from Penrith to Kirkby Stephen then up over the bleak and haunted moor of Stainmore to Barnard Castle and Durham. The railway and the Roman road, the Main Road we called it, were our links with the world on the other side of the fells which enfolded us like the arm of God. It was from the great wooden warehouse in the station yard that mysterious parcels, crates and boxes from Preston, Manchester, Birmingham, even London, were collected by the village carter for the shops; it was along the Main Road that the new motors first brought the strangers from outside.

But in the early twenties an influence more pervasive than the motors forced itself into our lives – wireless waves which, we were told, could penetrate the remotest valley and the thickest wall. There was no hiding from them, they were in the houses, the school, the church, the chapel, everywhere.

The motors and the wireless eventually reduced our mountain wall to a ripple on the earth's surface as, five hundred years earlier, gunpowder had condemned our chain of castles to a future as picturesque ruins.

But the Great War was the real watershed between the centuries of quiet, only penetrated over the previous seventy years by the friendly puffing and the occasional strident whistle of our four trains a day, and the daring world of the twenties and all that lay beyond.

I was born two years before the War on a snowy night in December 1912. The doctor lived at Appleby, the county town (it was really a large village) five miles to the west. At that time there was neither a motor nor a telephone in the village. The telegraph, operated by tapping out morse as in the old Westerns, was in the Post Office which was closed for the night. Anyhow the Appleby Post Office would be closed for the night as well so there was no point in trying to rouse our own postmaster. As my arrival seemed to be imminent, Jackie James, one of the two platelayers at the station, who lived next door, cycled through the blizzard to bring Dr Sprott. My father had never learnt to ride a bicycle and, in a village where everyone had to cycle to get about, I came to be a trifle ashamed of this.

The doctor came and I duly arrived without complications. He apparently said that I was a fine bairn but that I had a short neck and would probably be chesty when I grew up, a prophecy which is still unfulfilled.

Dr Sprott was an important and revered figure in my childhood and deserves a word in passing. He served a circle of country-side around Appleby of about forty square miles. The next doctor, Dr Bainbridge, served a similar circle around the village of Brough three miles to our east. It follows from the arithmetic that there was an overlap of one mile between the two practices and it was in this doubly served area that our village lay. As a result, some people had Dr Sprott and others had Dr Bainbridge. I never knew why we had Dr Sprott – we were certainly on excellent terms with Dr Bainbridge as well.

Those of us who had Dr Sprott were a minority and so we felt we were rather different and select and, as he clearly appeared to be further up the social scale than his rival who was of yeoman stock, we felt doubly select. Dr Sprott's origins were unknown. He was not local and that could be an advantage in those parts. Mystery about origins always attracts country folk. Moreover he lived in what was to us a big house where garden parties were held for good causes, and he kept servants who were dressed in the traditional black dresses with white aprons and white lace caps, all of which were unmistakable signs of gentry, even though the servants only got five shillings a week and their keep.

Looking back now he appears as a towering figure – though I believe he was slender and of medium height – always willing to make the five mile journey to see me when I got all the usual children's illnesses. With his greying hair, fresh complexion, penetrating eyes and tweed suits, he was a reassuring part of the little world in which I grew up.

He and the vicar were, I suppose, the first professional people with whom I came into contact. I regarded both with awe, admiration and a fair amount of affection. They and the gentry who dominated our community were, I quickly learnt, different from the rest of us in many ways; speech – never the 'thees' and 'thous' that we used, dress – Sunday clothes all the time, and different in life style generally, but perhaps the biggest difference of all was that they belonged to both worlds, the valley and 'ower t'top' as well. This gave them an indefinable aura in a village where hardly anyone apart from them had been to London and few had been further than Carlisle or Darlington or Blackpool.

The house in which I was born was one of fifteen, all totally dissimilar, which faced the beck. They were known as Main Street – though there was, as a matter of fact, no other. We called our house Brook View, a name which could have been equally applied to all fifteen, but I suppose we got in first when my parents were married on the first day in the twentieth century. Why 'Brook' I never knew. That was the posh word used by Shakespeare and Tennyson; to us it was invariably 'beck'. My father had a shop which was an integral part of the

15

house and took up a good deal of its cubic capacity, to my mother's perpetual annoyance. Our cramped living conditions might have been easier to tolerate had the business been highly successful but in the twenties it grew less and less successful. 'C. Short, Tailor and Draper. Agent for Pullars of Perth', the sign said, but with the coming of motor cars and, later in the twenties, the bus service, village people did more and more of their shopping in the country towns of Appleby, Penrith and Carlisle, where the choice was better though not the quality, and, as a consequence, the prices were lower. Village shops which, before the war were prosperous, began to decline throughout the valley and many disappeared. With the coming of ready-made, mass-produced clothes and bespoke tailoring our little business went down hill rapidly. Indeed it almost reached the point where the custom of a few local families kept it going. But my father, a pig-headed man, refused to deviate an inch from the quality clothes he had always provided nor would he lower his prices to meet the competition of the town shops. He had a rather pathetic belief that whatever happened there would always be people who were willing to pay for the best. The trouble was that there weren't enough of them.

And so my mother's not unreasonable view was that she was sacrificing a good part of her home to a business that barely provided a decent living. Fortunately, or perhaps unfortunately for her, we owned the house and shop as well as another cottage in which lived an old lady who, we had agreed, was to have it for life. The dwindling business and ownership of the premises anchored us there. We were in a state of inertia from which all my mother's fulminations, and they were pretty rough, could not extricate us.

Her complaint, 'we need a bigger house', was injected into every domestic problem, particularly those generated by her twin obsessions with cleanliness and order. And they really were obsessions, probably themselves caused by our limited living space. Her greatest abominations were dirt and untidiness. Whatever the cause of her obsession, she dusted daily where no speck of dust existed; she polished the already mirror-like surfaces; she blackleaded the kitchen range which was incapable of further improvement. Even the wooden beams in the living room ceiling had to be polished frequently.

Every day had its special activity, washing Monday, ironing Tuesday, baking Wednesday, bedrooms Thursday, living room Friday, and a grand recapitulation on Saturday morning called 'cleaning up for the weekend' which reduced the house to impenetrable chaos until mid-day. But after that the whole place sparkled and shone in splendour. Furniture polish, white gooey paste from a brown bottle, and newly baked bread are the two best-remembered smells of my childhood home.

All this cooking and baking was done on the kitchen range until we acquired a Valor oil stove, and all the washing in the set-pot in the washhouse, so fire-management was an important part of the domestic round. On baking day my mother pulled out the damper with the brass knob and removed the huge iron square at the back of the fire which covered the entrance to the flue under the oven. She then pushed into the flue a thick piece of wood two feet long and the flames could be heard roaring up the sides of the oven. As the oven stick burnt away it was pushed further in. A supply of them had to be ready for every baking day. Out of this primitive range she produced the most exquisite dishes and cakes which were renowned throughout the village.

Every week she baked seven or eight large white loaves of bread. She also made a number of basic cakes with occasional frivolities such as angel cakes. The never-failing weekly ones were rich brown ginger-bread in a huge tin, rock buns, pasties on plates using jam, rhubarb, gooseberries, apples, mince-meat, as well as minced meat and even egg and bacon for filling and – most delicious of all – huge oven cakes made by flattening the pastry on an oven shelf, spreading jam over it and then folding it over into a large sandwich.

On washing day my father had to light the fire under the set-pot and fill the boiler early in the morning. Here again sticks of a special size, thicker and longer than oven sticks, had to be ready to push in. Woe betide him and all of us if there was not a good supply ready. Washing day was the worst day of the week, a hated day, a day to get out at all costs, especially on wet days when there was steam, the smell of washing and ill temper everywhere.

The regular, clockwork predictability of the weekly round was suspended twice during the year. The first was for two weeks in the spring when the annual spring cleaning ritual was enacted. Even now, after all the years between, it is too painful to think about. It was a period of unrelieved chaos, of scratch meals, of bad temper, when every inch of every wall, floor, ceiling and all their contents had to be brushed, scrubbed, polished or painted. My mother was incapable of doing one room at a time. She believed it wasn't a thorough spring cleaning unless the whole house was dismantled and disorganized at once. But how it all shone on the eagerly awaited day when, by some magic, everything came into place again! I will not say it was worth all the misery, but it was part of the rites of spring and had to be endured.

The other annual disruption was the hearth-rug week which preceded a minor (but, none-the-less, nasty) 'back-end cleaning' in the autumn. Most families in the village possessed hearth-rug frames. These consisted of two $4'' \times 2''$ end pieces of polished wood about three feet long with slots at each end for taking the side pieces which were $3'' \times 1''$ and about five feet long. The hessian on which the hearth rugs were to be made was sewn around the end pieces and kept taut by winding most of it around one end and tightening it by means of nails stuck in a series of holes along the sides. The most intricate patterns were drawn on the hessian with chalk – many of them traditional designs based upon templates which had often been handed down from one generation to another. About two feet of canvas was available for working and the whole contraption was propped up on two trestles in the middle of the living room, where anyone, family or neighbour, who dared to enter during the week was expected to help.

There were two types of these excellent rugs – the looped ones which were used in the bedrooms and prodded ones for downstairs. Both were made from half-inch wide clippings of cloth from old clothes, and, in our case, from the seemingly endless supply of suiting pattern books. For prodded rugs the clippings had to be about three inches long. One end was pushed through with a wooden bodkin-like prodder and then the other end was pushed through near to it. This eventually produced a rug with a luxuriously thick pile which was ideal for the stone-flagged floors.

For the looped variety the clippings had to be long – any length. The tool in this case was steel pointed but with a blunt barb like a fish-hook. The clipping was pushed through the canvas, pulled back with the barb, pushed through again until it was used up. This produced a harder-wearing, carpet-like rug which was less pleasant to walk on but more prized than the prodded one, though I could never understand why this should be so.

Every cottage had a number of rugs which were rotated from the places where they got the least wear to where they got the most. They generally ended up at the back door and were discarded. A new one then came into use in the most special place in the house and all the others moved down one.

Behind Main Street and only about a hundred yards from the back of our house was Longstaff's wood-yard, an extensive joinery business and large saw-mill, into which newly felled timber was dragged under the jonker, two huge wheels on a long timber shaft beneath which the tree hung by chains and which was pulled by a horse. The word 'jonker' was probably a corruption of 'yanker' from the verb 'to yank'. As the new timber went in along the road between the beck and our house, brightly painted farm carts made with consummate skill, sheep feeding racks, hay rakes by the bundle, hen houses on wheels and all the other requirements of rural economy came out. The woodyard was a perfect adventure playground for us children, with great untidy piles of newly felled trees – rather sad looking fallen giants, stripped of all their finery and dragged humiliatingly from the quiet woods in which they had grown to maturity. In the large opensided drying sheds where we were allowed to play freely there were stacks of sawn wood of every conceivable size and shape. I can still distinguish most kinds of British timber not only by their colour and grain but also by their smell which requires much more skill. Among my earliest memories are the smell of drying oak and the high-pitched, agonized monotone of the great circular saw.

19

Even as a toddler I often peered into the sawmill itself and was always saddened by the final indignity suffered by a mighty tree as it was rent into planks and boards and posts. The flying sawdust which shot out in a stream below the sawbench was particularly sad – the shedding of a captured giant's blood.

And I categorized the ignoble end of noble trees with another great sadness I experienced early in my life – the killing of a pig which I watched at Row End Farm, a couple of hundred yards to the east. The great, lovably clumsy pig squealing with fear was manhandled by four or five farm men on to the killing stool and tied down by tight ropes which must have hurt it – they hurt my arms and legs to watch it – adding to the agony of its last moments. It looked very much like a tree waiting for its end on the saw bench as Tom Taylor the village pig-killer cut its throat with a knife whose sharpness was a legend. The dark steaming blood, like the sawdust, spurted out beneath into a bowl and we little boys, watching from the other side of the farm yard, turned pale and silent and felt very odd in our tummies as the squealing became terror-laden for a time then quickly faded away in dying gasps.

I found it hard to understand why tall, seemingly permanent trees, much bigger than a man, and friendly grunting pigs should be humbled and destroyed by strong and, it seemed, utterly remorseless men. They even laughed as they were doing it. I suppose like all young children I had a considerable capacity to identify with living things around me, indeed we were told in Sunday School that 'The Lord God made them all'. What these gruesome experiences of early childhood did to me I cannot imagine but I do remember having nightmares about them. After all, if this could happen to great trees and to pigs why not something equally terrible to me? 'Shades of the prison-house begin to close / Upon the growing boy', as Wordsworth put it.

It must have been about this period in my life that I adopted the practice common among children and primitive people, as well as some not so primitive, of following a simple and often quite ridiculous ritual in order to survive among all the dangers and hazards that seemed to threaten me. The ritual had to be the first one that entered my head, not the second or the third otherwise it wouldn't work. A long-used one was to touch three of the metal bars in the railings next door when first I went out in the morning. It was particularly important if I was going to school where the schoolmaster wielded his cane in a ferocious and (I thought) arbitrary way. At another period my heaven-dictated task – as I believed – was to walk backwards over the little bridge at least once every day. If I had been called in for the night and remembered I had not performed this task, I would make an excuse to go out by the backdoor, as though to the lavatory in the garden and then sneak along to the bridge. I knew that otherwise some dreadful fate would befall me in the dark night. If there were forces, as I was beginning to feel, which my parents, up to now my Gods, could not control I realized that I must develop my own magic to protect myself from them.

My pre-school days were the war years when the world was being turned upside down and many of my earliest memories relate to it in some way or other. In 1917 one of our village men who had been in the trenches when the Germans used gas, returned on sick leave unable to speak. A hoarse whisper was all that remained of the deep farm labourer's voice he had when he went off to the war. Here, I thought, was a strong man, a lord of creation, stripped of his voice, the very symbol of masculinity, by some people called the Germans. Others came back on crutches. They all wore their soldiers' uniforms – the flat hats and puttees I particularly remember because they were so different from anything I had seen before.

The adults too were vulnerable, it seemed, the men who had so callously dismembered the trees and destroyed the pig. The Germans must be even more powerful than the men in our village. This realization came as something of a shock, but we small boys did not just listen to the hoarse whispers of the gassed soldier with pale, frightened faces and queasy tummies. In this case we fought back! The war fever affected the children as well as the adults. No cowboys and Indians for us! The Western had scarcely reached us. The cinematograph man only came to the Temperance Hall once in a blue moon and usually with a few short comics or a Charlie Chaplin and a comic. So all our games involved fighting the Germans who lurked

21

around every corner, and every game ended up with the capture of Kaiser Bill. A few years later we were equally preoccupied fighting the Sinn Fein up hill and down dale.

Another remarkable phenomenon of the war years was a land girl, a laughing, big-bosomed lass in green jersey and fawn knee breeches who actually spread muck on the fields and did other jobs always believed to be beyond the range of farm women, who – oddly enough – did little work in the fields apart from helping at hay-time. She was, not unexpectedly, the object of intense interest to everyone and especially roused keen speculation among the farm men, many of whom fancied their chances with her, though she always held her own.

The war was brought nearer to Warcop when, as part of the village war effort, it was decided to accommodate a Belgian refugee family. Mary Alice Gregson from the shop had a vacant cottage which she made available – two up, two down, earth closet at the end of the row. Most families contributed something to the furnishing. My mother gave a hearth-rug, for our house was almost coming apart with hearth-rugs, and the gentry chipped in with bigger items such as chests of drawers.

The curiosity when the strange-looking, strange-sounding family arrived could not have been greater if they had dropped from outer space. All the village women made excuses to visit them to see how the foreigners ('but on our side, after all') lived. My mother was actually invited to tea with them and reported that they stood the cups on the plates and used the saucers as plates but that they seemed 'decent sort of folk' nevertheless. Soon settling down, they lived happily among us until the war was over.

About half-way through the war we stopped getting our weekly supply of farm butter. Every week my mother had walked to Blacksyke Farm, two miles down the Eden, to collect her two pounds of the deep yellow, salty butter they made there. I must have accompanied her often but my clearest recollection is of that last visit. Square basket over her arm, skirt daringly well clear of her ankles, she led me over the Eden, up across the high ground beyond, then down through the beech wood to Blacksyke, with the sun slanting through the trees into patterns of yellow light on the mossy floor of the wood. Arrived at the dairy, she asked for her butter, but when Mrs Frankland said the price had gone up to half a crown a pound my mother, in the outraged voice at which she was highly expert, said she wouldn't be needing any more at that price, and pointed out that when the war started butter had only cost 10¼d. However, the journey was not wasted, for it was a still autumn day and we gathered elderberries along the river on the way back. My mother was no mean wine maker and in the back-end of the year the summer's wine was always a major topic of conversation among the neighbours who gossiped with each other for hours on end. Warcop was a village of endless gossip. There was an annual ritual of tasting each other's vintage. It was sipped and sipped and sipped again, pondered over with wagging heads and compared with Nellie Richardson's of the year before the war or Mary Dent's of the year before that ('the year the war started' acting as the base line from which everything was dated).

So far as my mother's elderberry was concerned, *my* recollection is of a ghastly, foul-smelling witches' brew of high specific gravity and even higher alcohol content.

Of course those in the village who had been 'saved' wouldn't have such wine in their houses or even taste it, except for strictly medicinal purposes. We were among the 'damned', so when a passionate evangelist who was preaching at the chapel invited those who had been 'saved' to stand up, my father delighted in remaining firmly, immovably seated. And so at our house, being damned, we always had a stock of miscellaneously shaped bottles of wine, all neatly dated and kept in the large cupboard under the stairs called the pughull though nobody knew why. One of the minor excitements of life was when a cork blew out of one of those bottles in the middle of the night with a bang like a gun. 'The Germans have come;' I thought the first time I heard it. But when the whole bottle exploded, as one sometimes did, spattering the cupboard with glass and wine, it was an occurrence to be recounted for years.

Every Christmas we, brother, sister and I, received a huge parcel of presents from our older cousins, almost a generation ahead of us, in Carlisle. They were the most eagerly awaited presents of all, not only because our cousins spent more on them than anybody else including our own parents, but also because they usually used a good deal of imagination in selecting them. Unfortunately, in 1917, their imagination failed them! I had set my heart on a clockwork motor car with the winding key sticking out at the side (I had, indeed, wished myself into believing that their present was to be a car), and felt quite certain of it. Unfortunately, when the parcel was unpacked, it turned out to be a book of nursery rhymes with coloured pictures. No doubt it was a splendid book. Had I wanted a book this one would have been a perfect choice, but I didn't, I wanted a motor. In any case, I couldn't read. Quite inconsolable, I cried for ages about it without evoking any sympathy whatever from anyone and that added to my desolation. Looking back, I suppose I was fortunate to have got anything in that dark year of the war but I felt greatly and unfairly deprived. It was my first lesson that wishing does not make it so.

Each year there were at least two village Christmas parties – always called 'Christmas trees' – gloriously happy, slightly chaotic events. They were given by Lady Wynne and the Wesleyan Sunday School every year, once in a while by the Church Sunday School and, for a time by a couple who rented a house in the village and aspired to the status of gentry. They were always held in the Temperance Hall because there was nowhere else, and the same tree, a tall spruce erected on the stage and reaching to the ceiling was used for all of them, each donor providing different decorations and a wrapped and labelled present for every child.

The pattern was always the same – tea at 3 pm, on the long trestle tables with plates down the centre piled high with cakes and sandwiches, though the Wesleyans put each child's ration in a paper bag and I didn't like that a bit, then, candles lit on the tree, lights out and the presentation of prizes at 4.30. After the excitement of seeing what we had all got there were noisy and increasingly dusty games until 6.30. It was a miracle that we had no serious fire in the building with dozens of colourful, lighted candles in clip-on holders on the tinder-dry tree.

Neither Mrs Wild nor Mrs Chamley, numbers 1 and 2 in

the social hierarchy, gave a Christmas tree but Lady Wynne, who came next always did, and obviously enjoyed it, which gave her a special place in the affections of the village children. But it always surprised us that Mrs Wild and Mrs Chamley allowed her to get away with it. Perhaps there was a tacit agreement between them that, as there were two of them, they could ignore this affront to their status.

After the Christmas holidays of 1917 I started at the village school, a church school in the lane near the church. There were sixty-eight children from five to fourteen years of age in two rooms, a large one for standards two to seven and an Infants' Room for the little infants, the big infants and standard one. The Big Room, as it was known throughout the village, was heated by a huge coke stove which glowed red on cold mornings and smoked us out into the playground on windy ones. The Infants' Room had an enormous coal fire with an iron fireguard around it. The headmaster, who was the only qualified teacher, lived in the school-house next door but when I started he was away at the war as CQMS in Mesopotamia, an experience with which, when he returned, he never ceased to rivet our attention in every geography and history lesson and most others too. A succession of supply head teachers held the fort while he was away. Another teacher was 'uncertificated', which meant that she had passed an examination called the Queen's Scholarship, a grandiose title for the equivalent of the present day 'O' Levels. The infants were taught by a 'supplementary' teacher for which status the two qualifications were that she should be eighteen and vaccinated. All of which sounds pretty primitive but they were dedicated, competent teachers who effectively imparted the four R's (religion was the fourth) and a good deal else besides.

The Infants Room had four long pitch-pine desks with seats attached, two along each side of the room facing each other like choir stalls. The desks on the left of the fire were smaller than the others and I sat there as a new starter looking across the room rather nervously at the older ones of six and seven who surveyed me somewhat disdainfully from the wealth of their experience. The desk tops had ten inch squares divided into a hundred square inches, carved in the wood, at each place and underneath there was a shelf for personal possessions.

Half way through my first morning I asked to go to the lavatory, an earth closet across the yard, which always smelled of carbolic. But I didn't go, I ran home instead. Whether I had it all planned when I asked to leave the room or whether I cleared off home on the spur of the moment I do not remember, but I covered the half mile between school and home in no time at all. As I neared home I had a tremendous sense of freedom and elation. I knew nothing of the 1870 Act, nor of the inexorable power of the state to deprive little boys of their freedom, and to pursue me and bring me back. I was free and that was that. But, unfortunately, I was soon missed. Miss Robinson kept a close eye on us and a student teacher was sent to retrieve me. As I was led back into the Infants' Room I was one with the tree on the saw bench, with the pig on the killing stool. But this time I was not a spectator feeling vicariously for the victim: I *was* the victim. It was real, and there was no escape. My freedom was gone forever; never again could I wander around the woodyard in the mornings or play in Row End stack-yard in the afternoons, hearing the noise from the school playground across the meadow and able to exult in the fact that I wasn't there. I was bundled back into my seat defeated and humiliated.

However, in time, when I learnt to read and manipulate figures, I came to enjoy school. Life became easier when I learnt the rituals of both classroom and playground, for ritual and routine were extremely important in both play and learning. In no time at all I was chanting my tables as well as any of them —

> *two times two are four*
> *three times two are six etc.*

— in a monotone, except for the 'are' which was two notes up the scale. And in the gravel-covered playground I soon learnt:

> *The big ship sailed through the alley O*
> *Through the alley O, through the alley O,*
> *The big ship sailed through the alley O*
> *On the last day of September.*

There were also annual rituals such as the chant on Royal Oak Day:

> *The twenty-ninth of May is Royal Oak Day.*
> *If you don't give us a holiday we'll all run away.*

As far as I remember we never got a holiday but any child who was forgetful enough not to be wearing a sprig of oak got nettled on the knees by the older boys.

In those early years the days always seemed to be sunny and the nights dark, very dark. I find it difficult to remember a dull, wet day or a moonlit night. But the darkness of the winter's nights I shall never forget. No sooner had I got home from school and had my tea than it descended, enveloping everything like an impenetrable pall. Fields, trees, houses, the beck, all disappeared leaving me surrounded not by nothing but by mystery and menace. Hard as I tried, I could never accept my mother's assurances that there was nothing to be afraid of. How did she know – how *could* she know what dangers the darkness held?

My mother tried to reassure me because one of my chores from about the age of eight or nine was to go for the milk morning and night. In pursuance of her policy of spreading her custom, we got it from Row End farm in the morning – and I enjoyed going there – but from High Green farm in the evening and that in winter was a very different matter. It involved going to the other side of the village, up a dark road between high walls and then, after the last cottage, along a tree-lined, muddy path, over the stack yard to the farm house door. Often I had to wait in the byre, lit by the dim, yellow light of a stable lamp, until a pail of milk was available. It had then to go through the cooler before I could be served. I liked this delay because it postponed for a while the retracing of my steps back home. Even now I shudder when I remember the agonies I suffered in forcing myself along that path on dark nights. Sometimes I whistled, sometimes I almost tiptoed – as quiet as a mouse. I could never decide which was the safer thing to do.

There were no street lamps in Warcop and most houses were

badly lit, especially before our village electrification. What light came from them was screened from the outside by blinds which were always blue, and thick curtains. The lantern which was supposed to make my journey easier and remove all my fears cast a flickering glow over a radius of three feet around me. An owl, and there were many, looking down from the top of one of the trees would have seen a small yellow circle of light with a pair of boy's legs in the middle move up the path to the farm every evening. The knowledge that I was certainly being watched by the owls which always hooted when rain was coming, added to my fear — if that was possible. The image of a 'lantern unto my feet', a tiny area of comparative clarity and safety in a world of blackness, etched itself on my memory. Remarkable how, in adult life, we remember and try to resurrect the things that gave us comfort in childhood. But this image always evokes sadness as well as comfort. One tiny speck of humanity trying to repel the fringe of the fringe of that infinite cosmic blackness which envelops us.

Why my kind and loving parents subjected me to this nightly agony I find it difficult now to understand. My mother said it was to teach me not to be afraid of the dark! (as well as to get the milk). Unfortunately it had the opposite effect.

The most exciting and memorable event of my earliest years was something very different. It happened in 1918 when the son of one of our local gentry, Captain Merry Wynne, an RFC officer, landed his flying machine in a field near the school. Early one summer's evening it must have been, because I had not gone to bed. A gang of us younger children were playing near the beck when, quite suddenly, we saw a low-flying aeroplane, so low that we clearly saw the helmeted, goggled pilot looking out at us over the edge of the open cockpit. A plane of any kind was an event which brought all the people of the village on to their doorsteps but one which was flying just above the trees must be either a German spy plane or one of ours trying to land. We decided from the markings on it that it must be one of ours in trouble and we raced across fields and gardens in a hopeless attempt to follow it. But, after disappearing to the east, it reappeared lower than ever. Never before

28

had I seen such excitement in Warcop. The plane flew down the beck towards the river, dropping lower all the time. We were just in time to see it make a bumpy landing in a buttercup-filled old meadow on Eden Gate Farm.

By the time we got there it was waddling across the field towards us like a duck, its propeller still whirling, the pilot still wearing his goggles, now plain for all to see. When it finally stopped he took them off and jumped out. Then we were flabbergasted to see that it was Merry Wynne, the dashing young son of Sir Arthur Wynne who lived in Warcop. Had he come from Mars he could not have evoked more wonder and admiration. The *size* of his machine surprised us most of all, never having seen one on the ground before. How on earth could it fly?

By now most of the village people were converging on the field and approaching rather gingerly. The women stood about in small knots whispering to each other. We children scurried about, around and underneath the machine, examining every detail and listening open-mouthed when the co-pilot explained things to the men who, more daring than the women, had come nearer. Merry Wynne lifted me up to look into the cockpit and allowed me to work a switch, an ordinary, brass-topped domestic light switch, which was fixed to the dashboard.

For the next few days the life of the village revolved around the plane, indeed the life of the whole upper Eden Valley, for people came on their bicycles for miles to see it. But we locals acted very blasé when they came from our rival village of Brough pushing their bicycles across the field. After all, we had been there when it landed and had lived with it since. By now we were quite capable of explaining how it worked and, above all, it was a Warcop man who had flown it in. Those were ecstatic days. We were a superior race, superior even to Appleby, though it was the County Town with a mayor, the Assizes, twenty shops, two stations and a castle with a lord living in it. Appleby might have all this but it had never had a plane of any kind, let alone one flown in by one of its own people.

But our brief period of glory was soon to end. Fortunately, unlike the landing, we knew exactly when the departure was to be and the schoolmaster allowed us out of school to watch. They had some trouble in getting the engine to start. 'It's cold', 'it's wet', 'it's been sabotaged', we speculated. Merry sat in the plane while his colleague pulled down the blade of the propeller, a highly dangerous procedure, it seemed to us, but apparently the only way to start it. They shouted instructions to each other and after a good many splutters, each of which threatened to cleave the co-pilot in two, it roared into life. In the plane they put on their leather helmets and goggles and with this loss of their identity we felt bereft, we had lost our heroes. They were no longer our very own. With a cheery wave, an incredible noise and a barrage of foul-smelling exhaust they were off across the field to the far side near the river. After an about-turn there was a great roar and they began waddling back through the buttercups towards us but travelling faster than anything we had ever seen, faster than the motors on the Main Road. We were quite sure something had gone wrong and they would never get it off the ground but, just as we were becoming resigned to a crash of volcanic proportions the waddling stopped, the wheels had left the grass and up into the air it soared. In seconds it was roaring over our heads and circling a few feet above a row of oak trees near the school. We saw one of the fliers lean out and drop something which turned out to be a red, white and blue pennant weighted with lead. It had been made, we suspected, by Lady Wynne to commemorate this wondrous event in our lives, in hers and in the long history of Warcop. The pennant hung in the school for many years until there arose another Pharaoh who knew not our moment of glory.

But this daring young man who brought his flying machine to show it to his parents and his village was engraved for ever on the memories of the wartime generation of village children. To us he personified dashing youth, courage and daring of the kind that the war propaganda was continually glorifying. Ever afterwards when I tried to visualize ancient heroes such as Ulysses or King Arthur they always had the features of Merry Wynne.

News of the end of the Great War came through to the Post Office on the telegraph, and I remember seeing the Post Master running over the Big Bridge to tell our side of the village. After that the news spread like a bush fire. The church bells were rung by the vicar and the school was closed for the day. Three events marked for me the end of these early years.

First, at Habergill, where Sir Arthur Wynne lived at the base of the Pennines, we had a great bonfire for the ritual burning of the Kaiser. It was a cold, dark night, and I was wrapped up with two jerseys, somebody's long muffler and my overcoat. The excitement at being taken out 'after dark', the mysterious time which belonged to adults, impressed it on my memory. I do not think I had ever before been out of doors, or indeed, out of bed so late. It was like being taken into a strange new world, especially as the bonfire site was well out of the village and far beyond my playing range at that age. We had to go through the park behind the Hall where everything had unexpected and rather frightening new shapes. I held on to my mother's hand and was glad that almost everyone I knew was there with flashlamps or lanterns.

The fire was the biggest I had ever seen and, there on the top, sticking up grotesquely, was Kaiser Bill. He had been the bogeyman of all my early years and this was to be the end of him. The local farmers had assembled with their hay sleds a mountain of hawthorn and hedge cuttings and whin – the curse of these low foothills. And they had mounted a guard over it each night, a necessary precaution dating from an occasion before the war when someone had lit the Guy Fawkes bonfire two days before the 5th of November. My father always said the culprit was Thornborrow Richardson, father of Butcher Bob, who on a dark night had done it on his way home from the Joiners' Arms.

We stood around watching the blaze, looking like cardboard figures, orange and red in front and black behind. The bigger boys showed what to me was unbelievable daring in throwing back onto it the ends of branches which had partly burnt and fallen around the edges of the fire.

Never before had we had a bonfire away from the piece of waste in the middle of the village known as the playground. Never before one attended by almost everyone who could walk, including the gentry, who rarely attended to see Guy Fawkes disposed of, or, if they did, watched from a distance.

We stayed until only a low pile of bright, glowing embers remained and the Kaiser had gone leaving no trace. The savagery of the leaping flames which had reduced the towering pyramid to this state in such a short time dampened our excitement. What rather sobered me was, I think, this demonstration of another irresistible power unleashed by the tiny flame of one flickering match but, no sooner unleashed, than beyond the ability of my parents and all the grown-ups in the village to control. The tree in the sawmill, the poor old pig at Row End, the maimed soldiers, the law that said I must go to school, and now this fire. It seemed that my parents were not the omnipotent giants I had thought them to be in my toddler days but that they were beset by forces against which we were all powerless.

I had heard a good deal about 'hell-fire'. My family were omnivorous in their religious observance, even if not 'saved'. We went to both church and chapel probably because my father relied on both factions for his business. 'Hell-fire' often cropped up in the thirty-minute sermons of the local preachers as they banged the dust out of the purple cushion on the pulpit. Could this be what 'hell-fire' was like? Poor Kaiser Bill! – but then he deserved to go to hell. Throughout my childhood I believed the devil had a waxed moustache like him. Long afterwards the memory of the inside of our armistice inferno was a major deterrent which kept my feet – well, more or less – on the 'path of righteousness' about which I had also heard and which I imagined as the pleasant path, with primroses and bluebells which ran along the Eden through Willie Savage's wood. My straying from it was and still is, accompanied by the most appalling sense of guilt. And so, by one means or another, society ensures that its children are taught to conform.

In the early summer of 1919 Mrs Wild held a garden party at the Hall to celebrate the armistice and to raise money for the relief of the wounded. The stalls were arranged among the massive geometrical shapes of the carefully clipped yews and the whole proceedings were dominated, as you expected if you ever lived in Warcop, by Mrs Wild wearing a huge hat, exuding perfume to a radius of ten yards around her, carrying a white parasol and followed everywhere by two ugly, ill-tempered Pekes. She glided among the lesser folks in this golden setting like Titania, aged a little but truly regal still. The brass band played, the only music I had heard apart from our piano, the organs in chapel and church and my uncle's HMV gramophone with its huge horn. 'Blaze Away' and 'The Merry Widow' reverberated among the ancient trees and up towards the blue sky. There were tears in many eyes, bitter-sweet tears, when they played 'Roses of Picardy' and 'There's a Silver Lining'. For the grown-ups it was a day of both joy and sadness. There was a feeling in the air that, now the war was over, everyone could carry on where they had left off in 1914, but I think they all knew deep down in their hearts that this could not be. It was for our village, and for the world, the dawn of a new age. The leisurely safe old world had gone forever.

Still it was a rapturous day for us children. We ran over the springy lawns, poked the fat goldfish in the two circular ornamental pools, played hide and seek in the shrubbery behind the Hall and, generally, made the most of our time on what was normally forbidden territory.

However, the high point of the day for me was my win at the hoopla stall. The rings were, I expect, somebody's wooden curtain rings and, as such, slightly on the small side but, by sheer luck, I managed to land one cleanly over the top of a lead bust of Queen Victoria mounted on a black enamelled circular wood base. I cleared the head but not the base and so, according to a strict interpretation of the rules, I should not have had it, but dear, sweet old Lady Wynne (she must have been in her early forties but anyone over thirty was 'old') stretched a point and I became the proud possessor of a likeness of the Old Queen, as she was still called in Warcop. 'She has a high place in heaven', they said of her. To me my lead figure remained throughout my childhood a true *objet d'art*. Even in November 1922 when the Earl of Caernarvon and his colleagues opened the tomb of King Tutankhamun, I equated my Queen with some of the objects uncovered there. I knew every detail of her face, every jewel in her crown and every bump on her ample corsage. She was a unique possession; no child in the village had anything like her and I loved her dearly for all the years of my early childhood. The fact that the curtain ring had not fallen flat on the green baize table slightly impaired my joy of possession for a time, but it was quickly forgotten even by boys who had won nothing and I was left to enjoy the undisputed ownership of a rare possession.

But neither the bonfire nor the garden fête really ended the war for us. It was the erection and dedication of the war memorial that finally got it out of our blood stream and pushed it into history.

The controversy about the form our memorial should take was long and bitter. A majority thought a stone monument was a waste of money. In order to survive, we were of necessity a tight-fisted lot. One or two who had lost sons or lovers were especially vehement about it. 'Use the money for something useful', they argued. Our arch-rival, Brough, had decided to build a palatial Memorial Hall – with maple dance floor – what ostentation! But the gentry wanted a monument and, as they were meeting most of the cost, they had their way, and a site was selected on a small triangle of grass between the two bridges. The Lord of the Manor graciously 'gave' the land.

One afternoon we were playing in the beck near the Big Bridge when a huge lorry pulled up and started to unload the massive (to me they seemed massive) red sandstone blocks. Over the next few weeks they were to be closely examined by everyone. After all, this was quite an event in a village in which no new building, apart from the odd dutch barn, had been erected within living memory.

And we felt a close affinity with Whitehall where the Cenotaph was being erected. Warcop was having one as well as London. We were in the fashion.

The old retired men of the village watched critically every stage of the erection of our monument. Throughout the whole of my youth there always appeared to be a group of old men who were great talkers and walkers. They were a kind of village senate who discussed exhaustively, almost in the manner of medieval churchmen, every event, every occurrence, every change in the status quo both in the village and in the outside world. They argued about everything under the sun. I remember them spending a week discussing the direction in which the village of Tebay (now familiar to travellers on the M6) lay. In the end they borrowed an ordnance survey map from the schoolmaster and marked the direction in white paint on a huge glacial granite boulder which lay, and will lie forever, in the backyard of one of them.

But the building of a monument was something entirely new for them and it occupied them for weeks. They hung around the masons from morning to night. This stone wasn't plumb, that one was too heavy and was sure to sink; the vibration of the traffic would loosen the whole thing (there was not a single car in the village at that time!). But the monolith on top was the main target; it would never be safe with a narrow base like that. How the builders tolerated them I never understood.

Eventually it was finished, standing there in all its glory – its symmetry, its slap bang up-to-dateness, there for all to see, though some still doubted whether it was plumb. It gave us a new dimension to have a memorial standing in the middle of the village on the profane ground. Previously we had only had them in the churchyard or the cemetery. It conferred on us a kind of metropolitan status among the villages of the valley, Warcop and London! – though most places got a memorial eventually.

The dedication was a great and solemn day in the history of Warcop. The shops were closed, and everybody came except one woman who had lost a son and who remained implacably opposed to a monument. 'Lot of rubbish', she said as she ostentatiously scrubbed her front steps during the ceremony. The gentry in front, the rest of us behind, the vicar, the Rev. Seymour Shaw, officiated with his over-long surplice and moth-eaten college hood blowing in the breeze. His imperial beard after the fashion of Napoleon III was neatly trimmed for the occasion. The National Anthem, 'O God our Help in ages Past' and endless prayers dominate my memory of the ceremony.

But the poignant, ever-remembered moment came at the end when lovingly made wreaths and bunches of flowers were laid on the Eden gravel around the base. The names of the dead were on the east side of the plinth and among them was Lieutenant-Colonel G. G. Buckle DSO MC — Garry Buckle a popular, dashing man. His young and beautiful wife who lived at The Fox, a cottage over the beck from the War Memorial and who was related to the Chamleys at Warcop House, was there with her son Dickie, and her husband's parents. Great and obvious was Mrs Garry's embarrassment when 'old' Mrs Buckle stepped forward and kissed her son's name. It was a moment of drama and anguish such as Warcop, an undemonstrative place, had rarely, if ever, known before. For a moment the silence was intense and eerie. All the women present contrived to wipe their eyes without being seen and then the men found it necessary to blow their noses — very loudly to emphasize the fact that it was a perfectly normal thing to do on a cold day.

That kiss, a mother's passionate, ritual farewell to her lost one, was for me the end of the strange far-off happening, the Great War, which had swept away strong, seemingly impregnable men and maimed others from our previously secure little community. Sixty-four, one in ten, went to the war and eleven did not return. It was the end of Kaiser Bill and all his evil works. But it was also the end of a thousand years of isolation. Warcop would never be quite the same again. A car came bumping along the pot-holed road as we dispersed. We left our monolith standing erect in the centre of the ancient clutter of the village, our virile assertion that Warcop would live and thrive whatever the future might bring.

2

Us and Our Betters

Nobs

WARCOP IN THE TWENTIES was still a feudal pyramid with the Lady of the Manor sitting on the top like a cock on a farm-yard midden, and the tenant cottagers at the bottom of the socio-economic heap. Everyone had his place in the structure and knew it; few aspired to change their place and even fewer were successful in doing so. But we were an independent lot, everyone regarded himself as being as good as, perhaps better than the next one, not in an arrogant way but with a fierce belief that what he did was as important in the village as what anyone else did. The community was all important. Jack Watt, the rabbit catcher who came down from the fell each morning (when there was an 'r' in the month) with his bicycle festooned with rabbits, was as proud of his calling as the vicar and a good deal more successful with rabbits than Mr Shaw with sinners.

Every child (at an early age) learnt the Church Catechism by heart and the Diocesan Scripture Inspector, a dark-visaged priest called Arrowsmith, came to test us each year. Among other dimly remembered injunctions I learnt was that I must '. . . order myself lowly and reverently to all my betters . . . and . . . do my duty in that state of life, into which it shall please God to call me'.

Clearly the social structure was God's, or Cranmer's, creation and it would be down-right wicked to try to change it.

The feudal acceptance, hallowed by the Church of England, of an almost immutably fixed station in life for everyone, had as yet been barely touched by socialist egalitarianism, except perhaps among the railwaymen in the upper Eden valley who had contacts with their colleagues in Durham. But there was a strong, and old, Liberal tradition in North Westmorland.

The first Labour candidate did not appear until the 1924 General Election. He was R. P. Burnett, the son of a clergyman – which in itself shocked the local gentry beyond belief. What on earth was the world coming to! But he only polled 7,242 votes against Oliver Stanley's 17,935 – which reassured them! Incidentally I delivered leaflets for the Labour candidate in that election, my first involvement in Labour politics. Burnett's very appearance and that of his supporters ('a scruffy lot') let alone what they preached, infuriated the local gentry. 'The red rag brigade', Captain Jim called them when he took the chair for Oliver Stanley who represented the county from 1924 to 1945. The expression was the most derisory he could find on a public occasion. It was also the most offensive, for the excesses of the Russian Revolution were still fresh in everyone's minds. But it caught my imagination in a way he never intended. It gave Labour politics a glamour for me as a little boy which, oddly enough, it has never lost. A great marching crusade with a huge red banner flying ahead. Strange how a word, a sentence, a tiny straw can play a part in deciding the way we take.

Few young people except the sons of the gentry left the village to go to college. Outside their ranks one well-to-do farmer's daughter went to London University in the early twenties and got a B.A. This was regarded locally as a prodigious achievement. I believe she was the only one in the decade. The village school under an able though rakish headmaster with two assistants catered for everyone from five to fourteen. Secondary education for all and higher education for all who could profit by it were three decades and another World War away. Rab Butler was then an eighteen year old student at Pembroke College, Cambridge – Robbins was still at London University.

The opportunities for employment for boys were limited to what was available within a cycling radius of five miles which included the two small market towns of Appleby and Kirkby Stephen. The Railway, the Co-op and the Post Office, and for some, including myself, teaching, were the plum jobs, 'a job

39

for life and a pension after', they said. Failing these there was little apart from an occasional apprenticeship and the servitude of farm work – the last resort of every mother for her son. For girls there were one or two vacancies in shops in the market towns or going 'into service' in one of the 'big' houses in the village or elsewhere in the valley. A few of the more fortunate ones like my sister got into teaching. Apart from this there was nothing but farm work.

Yet it was still possible for the farm labourer who was prepared to endure years of almost monastic abstinence and saving to become a tenant farmer with a small place to begin with, probably worked part-time, but, eventually with 100–200 well stocked acres to hand on to his sons. Tom Grisedale whose dog Major killed my dog and whose sons were great wrestlers, was the local living proof that this could be done. The Almighty surely could not object, we felt, to such a small deviation from his scheme of things and, anyhow, it had been earned by years of skimping and saving, a major virtue in village values.

And so, because of our remoteness, because of the lack of opportunities for higher education and because of the limited range of employment there had been little erosion of social class. But in the early twenties there was at least a gentle breeze of change in the air. The returning soldiers who had roamed far and wide to places that had before the War only been pictures in school books brought back tales of Paris, of the pyramids and even of Babylon itself.

Motors were appearing on the Main Road in increasing numbers, indeed they could be seen almost every day by the beginning of the twenties and collecting numbers was becoming a major schoolboy pastime which greatly boosted Mrs Bainbridge's sale of exercise books. But the old men still believed that cars were just a passing fashion – that the horse would never be replaced.

Then the wireless brought the world into our valley. We actually heard King George speak! 'Just imagine hearing the King in Warcop!'

The tales and changed attitudes of the ex-soldiers, the coming of the motors, the wireless, all added up to something which could not leave the old order unscathed whether it was divine or not.

Meanwhile, the Lady of the Manor sat on the top of us all like a fairy on a Christmas tree and was determined to remain there whatever might be crumbling around her. She belonged to an old local family but her husband, who died of cancer in 1922, had been Registrar of the City of London Court for thirty-two years and long after his death she still spent the winter of each year in London, reappearing at the Hall with the early daffodils, usually with a newly recruited cook and housemaid. That was all the domestic help she could afford in the post-war years apart from local charwomen. The village boys always waited eagerly to see what the new servants were like; a new girl in the village was a rare and welcome event.

Mrs Wild was aquiline-nosed and wore lorgnettes. She dressed with a startling originality of both colour and design which, on the great village occasions approached sheer flamboyance. She was not tall but carried herself with enormous dignity. She took life very seriously and herself even more so. My dominant memory of her is of her nose, her large hats, her yapping, vicious Pekes, her perfume and her parasols.

Her son was always known as Captain Jim. Lacking titles the gentry contrived to use their army ranks, quite properly said Mrs Wild who had checked with the War Office. He had qualified as a barrister though it was said that he had never had a brief. He and his wife were as poor as church mice and lived on his mother, in a cottage called Dolly Hill outside the Hall gates. The local legend was that he had 'married beneath him' a hotelier's daughter from the south who was at first barely tolerated by his mother. However, she turned out to be both beautiful and charming and was eventually better liked than the rest of the gentry put together.

Mrs Jim formed and ran the Girl Guides shortly after the war and became known as 'Captain' to generations of village girls. The guides met in what had been the coachman's room behind the Hall, always on Tuesdays as every village boy who had ever lurked in the snowball bushes outside knew well.

Mrs Jim's other passion was for English country dancing and Morris dancing. Throughout the summer months she held a weekly session on the small lawn at the side of her cottage. Sometimes the piano was carried out through the french window but occasionally we had a fiddler from outside the valley who was said to be 'a bit sweet on her'. Looking back now, the rhododendrons and lilacs always seemed to be in bloom on these summer evenings – a horticultural impossibility! When, in June 1953 I sat in Westminster Abbey for those tedious three hours before the young Queen arrived and listened to 'Greensleaves is my delight' played, it seemed, endlessly I felt an overwhelming nostalgia for those lilac scented evenings, for the *Rigs O' Marlow*, for *Country Gardens* and for the beautiful Mrs Jim.

The Hall with its park and the adjoining High Green farm which was part of the small estate, gave Mrs Wild the physical control of a major part of the village, but she also asserted her manorial rights over all the waste land and wayside verges to which no one else laid claim. This included a half acre of damp ground in the middle of the village known as the playground on which stood the village maypole – a tall mast with weathervane on top, mounted on some ancient steps – and the place where the bonfire was built on 5th November.

She also claimed any timber growing on the waste land, as we discovered during the General Strike in 1928 when the village ran out of coal. This was quite serious for us, because all the cooking was done on coal fires or stoves except for the few fortunate families who owned one of the new Valor oil stoves. She decided, as her contribution to the alleviation of the general distress, to donate to various families some thick old willows growing along the beckside, provided they cut them down themselves. When my father asked if we could cut one down she wrote saying no – they were only for the really needy families. But he cut it down nevertheless – a minor challenge to her authority because of his permanent, unabatable fury at the manorial dues which every freeholder had had to pay her until they were extinguished by a lump sum payment.

She also owned the advowson of the village church and so the parson was her man. She claimed dubious ownership of the chancel and this gave her the privilege of entering the church by a small door near the altar and walking down the chancel to her pew in the nave which, of course, was the front one. The vicar dared not for his life start the morning service before she and her family had arrived. She never went to Evensong as the rest of the village did. That was strictly for the hoi-polloi. Captain Jim read one of the lessons in his clipped Harrow and Oxford accent which a few of the uppity ones in the village tried to imitate when they were trying to be very posh.

Because of her claim to the chancel Mrs Wild had it painted a different colour, not very different but different enough to make the point, old gold when the rest of the church was beige.

She was also Chairman of the School Managers and made rather grand periodic visitations, when a space would be cleared for her in the middle of the floor in the Big Room and the head-master's chair brought for her. When she was regally settled she checked the register and the log book, holding her lorgnettes by the handle with a well manicured and much ringed hand six inches in front of her eagle nose.

Every boy in the village had to touch his forelock to her. If we became lax in this a visitation was certain to follow a few days later and the headmaster was terrible in his wrath when we upset Mrs Wild. A major requirement for retaining his job was to keep her happy – a fact which he forgot to his cost some years later.

As you would expect she was Chairman or President of every other organization in the village except those connected with Temperance or Chapel. These included the W.I. which was started in the early twenties and in which she played a dominant, but strictly non-executive role, i.e. a role not involving work of any kind. Among other things she made available an outlying room in the Hall for the weekly cutting up of fish. This was a unique Warcop institution started by the W.I. in its early days. Fish was bought in bulk from a distant port and sent to us every Thursday by train. It was then cut up at the Hall and distributed around the village by another boy and myself. We had a rather sporty barrow, for quick delivery, made from a tea chest and two bicycle wheels with tyres. We took the smelly, newspaper wrapped parcels to each W.I. member, collected the money and paid it to the Secretary, a minor but much loved one of the gentry who lived in another cottage between the two big houses.

But Mrs Wild's greatest village interest in the post-war years was neither the school nor the W.I. but the Sports Club. When Captain Jim finally had to leave London and come home to live abstemiously with his wife, he persuaded his mother to allow him to start the club in the rather breathtakingly beautiful park behind the Hall. Almost an acre of flat old pasture land was fenced in and an ancient but highly efficient mowing machine and roller from one of the big houses produced two excellent tennis courts and a cricket pitch in no time at all. There was an enormous amount of expertise about lawns in Warcop.

Every evening throughout the long summer the tennis courts and cricket nets were occupied until dusk. Captain Jim came down from the Hall after dinner, always wearing his slippers, and taught anyone he could get hold of all he had learnt at Harrow and Oxford about cricket. If a boy did not keep a straight bat or took his eye off the ball, his language turned the evening air blue, but his enthusiasm for sport and the time he devoted to it – for he had absolutely nothing else to occupy him – gave Warcop in the twenties respectably high standards in cricket, tennis and football. We could more than hold our own in the weekly matches against other villages. The biggest cricket match of the season was played against Temple Sowerby every August Bank Holiday. Play started in the morning and there was a long lunch break when everyone walked over the park to the Railway Inn where Mrs Walker, the landlord's wife, provided a gargantuan meal.

I and a number of other boys kept the score book and hung up the metal numbers on the pavilion as the game progressed. But in the late twenties the most sought after perk of the scorer was to be selected to go to one of the away matches with the team, all twelve of us packed into the huge old hire car owned by Jack Walker, the son of the Railway Inn. My mother was much less keen on this, as she thought – quite rightly – that I would hear lots of things I shouldn't.

The club also attracted a number of village handymen notable among whom were Jim Hodgson, the blacksmith's assistant, who acted as groundsman and Ephraim Allison, a retired police superintendent, whose wife created our Warcop *haute couture*. These two gave most of their spare time to the Club for many years, keeping the ground in order, building the pavilion, erecting seats for spectators, putting up fencing, all of which gave us the best provided Sports Club in the Eden Valley. As with the village pantomime, when the gentry were involved everybody co-operated.

And so the position of Mrs Wild as our great lady was supreme and unassailable and accepted, or mainly accepted, by the next family down the hierarchy, the Chamleys. They, by coincidence, were also a mother and son, Captain Tim, who lived in Warcop House, the second biggest house, just below the Hall. The Chamleys were not really gentry, though they thought they were and we accorded them the status. They were in fact descended from a Kendal miller who had nine children the youngest of whom came to Warcop to farm the rather bleak Moor House farm beyond the Main Road. But two or three generations transformed a farming family into at any rate a passable imitation of gentry.

Old Mrs Chamley and Captain Tim were a genial, good-natured pair who, like the Wilds, still kept up appearances though wartime inflation and post-war deflation had greatly diminished them.

Also like the Wilds, the grounds around their house were immaculately kept by another gifted gardener, old Robert Beetham (the prefix old was widely used and implied, as well as 'getting on in years', an element of affection). Old Robert was the patriarch of Warcop's most prolific and handsome family. There were four roads into the village and there was one of his married sons or daughters strategically placed by each one to keep an eye on all comings and goings.

Mrs Chamley used to drive around the country lanes daily in a governess cart, straight as a ram-rod beside a top-hatted Robert, black wheels gleaming and flashing in the sunlight behind the well-groomed flanks of her white horse. This was the horse, an ill-tempered brute, that later killed young Ernie Beetham, Robert's grandson.

Mrs Chamley was a Queen Maryish figure, indeed she looked

the part of Lady Bountiful much more than the Lady of the Manor. I always suspected she was aware of this and was secretly amused by it though she, like the rest of us knew her place and kept it.

Both she and Captain Tim ranked for a touch of the forelock. There might be uncertainty about whether some of the minor gentry qualified but there was none so far as the Wilds and the Chamleys were concerned. Salute, or you were in trouble with the schoolmaster! But the two Chamleys always returned the greeting with a cheerful word and a charming smile, though anyone who got a grunt out of mother or son of the Wilds was lucky. *Mrs* Jim was a different matter: she was everyone's friend.

Captain Tim had as little to occupy him as Captain Jim. Neither had an estate worth mentioning to look after. The Wilds owned two farms, High Green adjoining the Hall grounds and a farm at Burtergill below the fells; both were let to good tenants. The Chamleys had sold most of the land they owned in the post-war property boom. Both had excellent gardeners and so, apart from lending a hand with mowing the lawns and a little gentle topiary work at the Hall, the two gallant captains were completely without occupation of any kind though both were still reasonably young. They fished a little, shot an occasional pheasant or partridge but apart from this, a daily drink at the Railway Inn and an occasional game of cricket there was nothing for them to do except, of course, to provide companionship for their mothers, both of whom doted on their sons. It was a mark of our lingering feudal languor that in a village where hard physical work was the lot of almost everyone no one criticized the idleness of these two amiable gentlemen.

Their mothers were the two pillars of our community and their sons were there to support them, the four of them providing the corporate leadership of the village in spite of a mild, good natured (on the Chamley side at least) rivalry between the two families. This state of affairs, even in the heady immediate post-war years, was still regarded as the natural order. And it had its points. They cared for the place, the village was permanently in a state of order and tidiness

46

which, had it still existed fifty years later, would have carried off the Best Kept Village prize. They had the time, money, ideas and premises to generate village activities and, indeed, they felt an obligation to do so. They provided a head of steam for church, school, reading room (not the Temperance one!), sports club, Guides – for everything. They were the axis on which we rotated and, at that time, paradoxically, a village community still needed an axis. Paradoxically, because we were thrown on our own resources a great deal. Our self-reliance was seen especially in the way in which we had to provide our own entertainment at home, sing-songs around the piano if you were 'church' – but organ if you were 'chapel' – cards, dominoes, chess, draughts, ludo, snakes and ladders, fretwork and a host of other pastimes which involved activity of hand or brain. Yet we could only function as a community with the leadership of the nobs.

But to return to Captain Tim who had at least an absorbing hobby, he was a dedicated and highly expert ornithologist with the best collection of birds' eggs I have ever seen. Probably it was the last great collection of British eggs which will ever be assembled as collecting is now illegal. It is still preserved, in Tully House Museum in Carlisle.

Captain Tim showed me his eggs, with almost schoolboy enthusiasm on a number of occasions. I was always enthralled as much by the huge rooms, the thick carpets and, what then appeared to me to be, the luxurious mahogany cases with drawer after packed drawer of eggs, a far cry from my poor collection on cotton wool in cardboard shoe boxes.

When I went home our living room seemed like a tiny cell after being in Warcop House. What bliss it must be, I thought, to have as much space as that to live in – and only two of them! From those days of early childhood in a tiny house I have always believed that of all the deprivations to which children are subjected, to be deprived of adequate living and playing space is one of the worst.

Third in the Warcop pecking order came our celebrity, General Sir Arthur Wynne G.C.B. who had been a General in the Boer War. He had married a local girl related to the Chamleys and, in 1911, became the Keeper of the Jewel House in the Tower of London. We felt very superior when we reminded people from other, lesser, villages that of course we had in Warcop the Keeper of the Crown Jewels and the Registrar of the City of London Court. Come to think of it, it *was* rather remarkable.

Sir Arthur built himself a house above one of the beautiful gills which pierce the lower slopes of the fells. Embodied in it were doors, staircases and other fitments which had come out of the Tower of London and which had been brought all the way from London by rail. 'Fancy using all that old second-hand stuff' the locals said. The fact that a remote house in the northern Pennines was associated in this way with Britain's most historic building did not occur to us. We simply thought he must be an old skin-flint who was building his house on the cheap. But it turned out to be a quite beautiful house. He laid out the gardens with taste and a good sense of proportion and it was eventually and rather reluctantly, accepted by everyone except the other gentry, as a proper gentleman's 'place' with a long drive, oak gates and a cottage for a housekeeper. And what other signs of a toff's house could anyone want?

Sir Arthur was a morose looking old man with a drooping walrus moustache. Probably he was not old at all but he seemed so to me. Yet he was always willing to give to local causes. He once gave me a ten shilling note − a splendidly generous donation at that time − towards a fund for purchasing new cricket equipment for the school and wrote his name, 'Arthur Singleton Wynne', in a firm hand at the head of the first page in the blue school book in which I was to enter the subscriptions.

Looking back, I think I displayed considerable tactical skill in asking him before anyone else, for none of the other gentry could possibly be outdone by him. After all he was only third in the scheme of things. As a result, the appeal succeeded beyond the wildest dreams of the schoolmaster and we got our new bats, balls, pads, wicket keeper's gloves, etc.

Sir Arthur owned a white fell pony and often rode up into the fells behind his house to shoot. He was a squat determined little figure with deer-stalker hat, legs dangling by the fat belly of the pony as he plodded alone up the sweeping grassy slopes to find the grouse on the high plateaus which separated our valley from the upper reaches of Teesdale. One could well imagine him leading his troops across the veldt.

One dark winter's day the fog came down and he had not returned when darkness fell. Lady Wynne raised the alarm in the village and in no time at all a rescue team was organized including my father and my brother. They climbed up the fells to the bog-pocked plateau on the top with a miscellaneous assortment of stable lamps, candle lanterns (these were highly efficient) and flash-lamps. But the night was so dark, the fog so impenetrable and the distances so great that he could not be found. They searched, shouted and whistled until morning when word came that he had been found near Cauldron Snout on the Tees by Edward Mason of Birkdale Farm — reputed to be the loneliest dwelling in England — and was being looked after there. Eventually all the members of the team were presented with inscribed knives which were long cherished as mementoes of a night which has passed into village history, but to Edward Mason he gave his white pony complete with its panniers. When I camped at Birkdale years later the rescue of Sir Arthur was still a favourite topic of conversation.

His wife was one of the sweetest, kindest women I remember. She was effusive, 'flarchy' the village women called her but she was always friendly and interested and tried to help according to her lights. In the great flu epidemic of 1918, which caused more deaths than the Great War, my father almost died, and I remember Lady Wynne coming to the house with some jugged hare in a milk can which, she said, was the very thing to build up his strength again. Almost a caricature of Lady Bountiful — but a kindly act nonetheless.

It was typical of her cheerful attitude to life that she nicknamed two of her sons Merry and Gay. It was Merry who had landed his plane near the school during the war.

She lived on into the 1950s, the sole survivor of all the gentry who had dominated our lives half a century ago. God rest her gentle soul.

After the Wilds, the Chamleys and the Wynnes the pyramid widened. There were a number of minor gentry, mainly rather indigent, elderly or middle-aged, relatives of the top ones, living with whatever style they could muster in cottages full of antique furniture and cared for by able cook-housekeepers.

Miss Irving, a bright and busy little woman, inseparable from her two West Highland terriers, which had a long standing blood feud with Mrs Wild's pekes, devoted her life to the Women's Institute and her garden. She was loved by everyone except the postmaster who loved no one except his family.

There were also two middle-aged spinsters, the Miss Hills. Milly was tall, lanky, masculine and walked like a farmer; Nellie was short, plump and waddled like one of our India Runner ducks.

They took over the cottage belonging to Row End farm and quickly set about transforming the messy garth in front into a quite delectable garden, complete with stream and rustic bridge and stocked with perennials from the gardens of Warcop House. What had been a plain farm cottage was quickly gentrified with french windows opening onto a paved terrace complete with an aviary of cooing doves. But the great achievement was the garden – mainly the work of Milly who was our local version of Gertrude Jekyll.

Milly, the lanky one, also made good a deficiency about which we were rather sensitive, especially when talking to the people of the village of Brough – our major rival in the valley. We had Guides and Brownies but no Scouts. Dear old Milly persuaded Captain Tim to let her have an empty cottage near our house and formed the 1st Warcop Troop. She taught us woodwork, leatherwork (toggles galore), and basket work but, above all she taught us to enjoy singing which was a new experience after the murderous tonic solfa sessions at school. 'Excelsior' was her favourite and we up-pi-deed at the top of our voices until the rafters shook. It was all very Boys' Own Paperish but we loved it.

Milly was a roaring success as a leader of little boys and she looked the part in her B.P. Scout hat, with her white lanyard and whistle around her neck, her tweed ankle-length skirt, woollen stockings, brown nobbly shoes and shooting stick.

Though the Guides thought it very odd that the Scoutmaster should be a woman – and the Brough Scouts hooted their heads off about it – we never really thought of her as such. She was one of us and could do all the things that we could do – or most of them.

Of course her patrons were the Chamleys to whom she was related, but the Guides had the patronage of Mrs Wild and that gave them the edge on us. And so an on-the-whole friendly rivalry between the top two families was extended to the two youth organizations. But that did not worry us in the least.

Another cottage, called The Fox because it had once been a pub, was occupied by the young war widow, Mrs Garry Buckle, who was also related to and under the patronage of the Chamleys. Her husband had been the son of our second General who owned the Old Cottage in which Miss Irving lived. Mrs Buckle lived at The Fox with her young son Dickie who was born in 1916 and his Nannie. Dickie was to become Britain's foremost ballet critic, the biographer of Diaghilev and, more recently, the latest arbiter of what is U and what is not.

Although we recognized them as gentry, Dickie was surprisingly allowed to play with me under the broad sandstone arch of the big bridge opposite The Fox where the water was only ankle deep and where we caught minnows and chased the ugly bullheads and tommy loachers from stone to stone. This was a clear breach of one of the social understandings in Warcop. The young of the nobs never, never played with the young of the commonalty. Polite to each other they might be – but nothing more. Mrs Wild had two pretty granddaughters who stayed with her most of the summer and the Chamleys had a most attractive niece called Vera Woodburn who stayed with them from time to time, but fraternization was unknown, which was a pity because all the village boys who were old enough to appreciate such matters fancied them a great deal.

In the early twenties a well-to-do family called Shorrock settled in Warcop. Mr Shorrock and his wife bought and renovated a pleasant Georgian house called Eden Gate and his sister took a furnished cottage. She and her brother were reputed to be very rich, their wealth being assumed from the numbers of servants they employed and the amount they spent

51

on modernizing Eden Gate – a fairly accurate barometer of wealth. Compared with our gentry they were obviously well-off and for this reason they were the targets of a number of barbed comments. We were not all that fond of our own gentry but we rather resented anyone making them look poorer than they were. When Mr Shorrock was ill – 'No wonder', said Mrs Wild 'the colour of the house would make anyone ill.'

But Miss Shorrock who had been to Oxford, quickly found a niche in the hierarchy and became active in village affairs. Among other things she took over the cubs from Milly Hill – another huge, tweed-clad, lumbering figure among her little boys. As she became familiar to the children she naturally became fully accepted by the village as one of our gentry.

In fact, after a few years of good works, a remarkable thing happened. She fell in love – with Captain Tim – and he with her. Everybody was astonished though the knowing ones said they had 'seen it coming'. But how could two of the gentry, getting on in years or so I thought, fall in love, especially when they were so set in their ways that you could almost set your clock by Captain Tim's daily activities? Falling in love was something only ordinary people did. Nevertheless it happened and their engagement was announced.

Eventually they were married and the new Mrs Tim moved into Warcop House, all of which we observed, by applying our infallible criteria, revived the Chamley fortunes no end. The number of servants doubled from two to four, an assistant gardener was taken on, the house was freshly painted in gleaming cream and improvements appeared everywhere. Most exciting of all, a gleaming new motor, a saloon, replaced the governess cart, the stable in Robert Beetham's yard was converted into a garage and the vicious white horse was pensioned off.

It was not lost on any of us that the new Mrs Tim, who had the Warcop passion for gardening, had two ornamental pools constructed in the grounds – not one but two – and that there were two pools at the Hall. Indeed the reinforced Chamley fortunes looked like disturbing the balance of power between our two top families. But Mrs Wild, confident that her position was unassailable ignored the changes with, on the whole, good grace.

But the car was something she could not allow to pass unchallenged. It was after all *the* symbol of the new post-war age and if Lords of the Manor were to survive they must keep up with the times. Within weeks of the appearance of the Chamley car a brand new saloon appeared at the Hall and Willie Watt the gardener was dressed up like a Ruritanian general in a smart brown uniform to drive it. The Hall was not to be outdone – two ponds and cream walls indeed!

Neither fish, flesh nor good red herring

The vicar clearly did not belong to the gentry, not even the group of minor ones but, equally he could not be placed among the well-to-do farmers and shopkeepers. He was the educated man which it was once thought to be the function of the Church of England to provide for each parish. He had no trace of regional accent and this alone would have made him pass for an educated man in a village where the broad Westmorland dialect made us almost incomprehensible to outsiders. He really was, however, a well read, well informed man.

He lived in a large, extremely beautiful but internally inconvenient, vicarage and kept one maid. He dined occasionally with the gentry and ran a two-seater car with a dickey seat at the back – one of the first in the village. The original idea of the dickey was as a seat for a servant.

All this should have aligned him with the Wilds, the Chamleys, and the Wynnes and all their relatives, yet he sent his children to the village school, an unheard of thing for gentry to do. And this was not due to any egalitarian philosophy, for he was just as Tory as the gentry.

But the thing that really made it impossible to place him was his poultry farm which he developed from the keeping of a few hens in the war years to a large enterprise filling most of the glebe fields around the vicarage. This he did entirely with his own two hands and the help of a certain amount of child labour. Now the gentry never, ever engaged in manual work if the purpose was to make money; they would slave away in their own gardens but to do it for gain would have seemed unutterably vulgar. So Mr Shaw and his family were socially *sui generis*, not fitting in comfortably with either the upper or the lower stratum. Yet perhaps they were none the worse for that since it gave them the invaluable role in the village society of providing a bridge between the gentry and the rest of us.

In his early years at Warcop he kept a donkey which died just before Christmas in one of the early years of the war. When the carol singers visited the vicarage that year they were invited into the kitchen and given bowls of soup in which were floating large chunks of meat which defied identification. There was a double mystery – what was it and how had the vicar come by so much meat in wartime? Then somebody remembered the donkey! The story of the donkey soup passed into Warcop folklore and is still vividly recalled by the few survivors of the carol singers of sixty-five years ago.

After the war the vicar began with tremendous energy to develop his poultry farm into a lucrative enterprise. His stipend was low, only £400 p.a. – even after he had persuaded a local lady to make a bequest to increase it – and his parochial duties were light, but the real reason why he loved his hens was that he was an outdoor, practical man who gloried in using his hands.

After the war he bought huge ex-army huts from Gretna and had them transported to Warcop and converted so that each one housed a hundred or so white leghorns – free range, of course. Intensive methods of egg production had not then been thought of.

From the early twenties I spent a great deal of time with Mr Shaw, sometimes hoeing the border of the churchyard beneath the magnificent yew hedge – one of the best in the county until Captain Jim cut it down. At other times we would work together in the huge kitchen garden which had medieval masonry just below the surface. But most often I would help him with the poultry – turning the eggs in the incubator, feeding young chicks, holding up endless rolls of wire-netting while he knocked in the staples or, my least favourite job, scraping the dropping boards. Although I suppose over the years of my childhood I provided him with a vast number of boy-hours of labour (he usually paid me 6d. a session) he always worked side by side with me and I greatly enjoyed his company. His academic achievements had not been outstanding but he was a studious man. This always surprised me when he was also so intensely practical.

Each Sunday he preached two twenty-minute sermons which, while far from gripping, were always well researched and interesting. Indeed they were so good that it was rumoured by his detractors (and he had some) that he bought them for £1 a dozen.

Village people had, and still have, a habit of making up their minds before looking at all the facts about a situation and then doggedly defending their prejudice. My long, long talks with the Rev. Seymour Shaw over my formative years taught me much but especially objectivity. He always refused to praise or blame, condone or condemn without weighing one side against the other, and I shall always be thankful to him that perhaps a little of that rubbed off on me. Indeed I remember consciously trying to imitate him, and what greater praise could any parish priest expect.

The only time I ever saw him talk passionately was on a famous occasion when the village gossips had been taking someone's character apart. He announced that he was going to preach about them at Matins on the following Sunday and, my goodness he did! He lambasted them with a fury which was the verbal equivalent of driving the money-lenders from the Temple. It was a sermon the like of which had not been heard in Warcop Church in living memory.

He was tall, dignified and gentle, but he was something of an introvert. He maintained long periods of silence as we worked together, but at other times he talked freely about everything under the sun. He always wore clerical grey and, no matter how hot the day or the job, never removed his clerical collar, though occasionally he would take off his jacket and hang it on a fencing post.

His poultry farming activities became so extensive and demanding that he could not have devoted much time to the pastoral care of his scattered flock but he was well-liked and always seemed to be there in an unobtrusive way when anyone needed help.

If I had been particularly useful to him, he and his wife, a jolly but brutally abrupt woman, would take me to Carlisle, on their Saturday jaunt, in the dickey seat of their car. When we arrived in Carlisle market place my long black, anarchical hair would be sticking out at right angles making me look like a golliwog and I would be frozen to the marrow but exhilarated as never before.

The main purpose of the trip was to buy nails, staples, bolts, and all the other hardware he needed on his farm — most of which was bought at Woolworth's. After that came the highlight of the day, lunch at the Silver Grill which was the first restaurant I was ever in.

These trips and my close association with Old Shaw (as we always called him) lasted until I left the village to go to college in 1931.

I have always marvelled at the fact, and it was a fact, that this very earthy country vicar who was not at all religious, who saw his pastoral function as being available if he was needed and called upon, whose priestly functions were performed at the minimum level which complied with the Thirty-Nine Articles — by which he set great store — should have been perhaps the major influence on me up to my late teens. Yet so it was and I always remember him, if not with warmth, at least with gratitude and affection. Perhaps it was because he treated a growing boy without condescension.

Farmers

After the gentry the most clearly defined and powerful social group were the farmers — five in the village itself and another twenty-two in the rest of the scattered parish. When they asserted themselves they were perhaps more influential than the nobs. Some were tenant farmers and others owner-occupiers but all were believed by the non-farmers to have 'plenty of brass'. This belief was obviously well-founded in the case of such sturdy characters as Robert Lambert, tenant of a hill farm at Burtergill, one of Mrs Wild's two farms, who also owned two other farms in the village.

Mr Lambert was a jovial, modest little man and generally regarded as the doyen of the farming community, at least of the Church half of it, for the farmers could be divided into two categories, the Church — Conservative-Reading Room ones who drank a little, played whist a lot and generally exhibited, to a tolerable degree, the common weaknesses of mankind. The others were the Chapel-Liberal-Temperance Institute ones who neither drank nor played cards and who exhibited the common weaknesses to a somewhat lesser degree.

It was equally beyond doubt that Alf Ellwood was well heeled. He was a jolly, Batesian character who owned and farmed Row End as well as dealing extensively and profitably in cattle. Nor could there be any doubt about the Franklands of Blacksyke on the Eden or about the Wilkinsons at the second farm at Burtergill. Least of all were there doubts about the appropriately named Jimmie Brass of Mere Banks who was said to be very wealthy.

When Jimmie got his car it was delivered to the farm and he asked the men who brought it to put it in the field near the house so that he could 'have a go' after milking. He studied the instructions carefully and had no difficulty in getting it started. With Jimmie clinging to the wheel it shot across the grass at a great pace but, unfortunately, his excitement was so great that he couldn't remember how to stop it and had to circle the field until the petrol ran out. At least he knew how to steer by the time the engine finally stopped.

Most of the farmers probably had a struggle to make ends meet. Their farms at that time required at least four times as much labour as they do today, miserably under-paid though it was. £20 for the half-year with board and lodging was regarded as a fair wage for a farm worker in his early twenties and £10 for a boy in his teens.

But, compared with the cottagers, all the farmers passed for rich or semi-rich with their large farm houses and a plentiful supply of home-produced food – potatoes, swedes, bacon, eggs, milk, butter and poultry.

All were intensely conservative, though they tended to criticize the gentry in, to say the least, quite radical terms. In fact there was a permanent tension between the two groups, not a destructive tension but more of a wholesome mutual respect which, at the edges, shaded into rivalry in maintaining their respective positions in the village community. Apart from the two farms owned by the Lady of the Manor and the odd field or two belonging to the Chamleys the Warcop gentry were virtually landless – but the farmers owned or rented the greater part of the parish. This control of the land counterbalanced the mansions, the uniformed servants, the gardeners, the posh accents, the airs and graces amd all the other marks of gentry and, in doing so, preserved a kind of social equilibrium.

Some of the farmers were pillars of the church and others of the chapel. Some, like Bill Bird of Eden Flat, who was my father's special friend, avoided both. He said he was going to hell and didn't care! There was, for example, Willie Savage a middle-aged bachelor who lived with his widowed sister, nephew and niece at the Tower – the oldest farm house in the parish, which he owned. He was strong chapel and, to me as a child, was what I imagined a saint would be like – quite unlike my hero, the poultry farming vicar. He had never been known to touch 'strong drink' or to raise his voice in anger. He was the superintendent of the Wesleyan Sunday School and leader of the Band of Hope which was his special pride and joy. We all joined, principally because of the annual 'de-monster-ation' (as we called it) which was held at one or other of the two country towns on either side of us. It was a memorable day in our calendar with an early train to the venue, a very slow and boring march to the field with bands and banners, a picnic on the grass, the crowning of the Temperance Queen and then all the fun of the fair.

There were also the magic lantern shows four or five times a year when we sat on the hard forms in the Temperance Hall and watched a succession of tear jerking stories of how a happy, smiling marriage had been destroyed by the Demon Drink.

Magic lantern shows were extremely popular in the village from the late nineteenth century to the early twenties when they began to lose their attraction to the growing popularity of the itinerant cinematograph. But *Show Boat*, *Sonny Boy* and the stream of talkies which followed killed them stone dead.

The magic lantern had a powerful acetylene light which fizzed all the time and smelt appallingly. The slides were brilliantly coloured and were produced in studios by profes-sional artists. The temperance movement used them as their most effective visual aid to drive home the evils of strong drink – it was always 'strong' drink – and they must have made a considerable impression on us. How could I ever forget the story of little Nell (or was it Jess), and the scene where she lay in bed about to expire. There, in a squalid room from which most of the furniture had obviously gone to the pawn shop, she was making her last desperate plea to the drunkard father who had brought her to this pass, to give up the demon drink, while a group of angels waited at the other side of the bed to take her soul away? And the look on her face so clearly meant that all would be forgiven if he did so. Or how could I forget the widow driven out into the snow at midnight by her paralytically drunk husband and clutching her emaciated babe to her bosom – or the orphans left alone, hungry and friendless in the all but empty house? The message was always loud and clear – total abstinence, nothing less. And in this the movement was wise, for total abstinence is always easier than moderation.

We also sang the Temperance songs. There was one in particular which we always enjoyed because it involved one of the great wonders of the twenties, the motor. The chorus went:

On foot I trudg'd it wearily when in the drunkards' school
But now I seem to ride alway for Temp'rance is my rule.
I'm glad I entered on the track to have a car so fine,
For now I drive to town and back in this handsome car of mine.
Merrily O! I drive away! drive away! drive away!
Merrily O! I drive away! in my teetotal car.

We were conditioned outrageously by singing at Warcop. The schoolmaster taught us to sing patriotic songs, Miss Hill, the scoutmaster, manly songs and Willie Savage, temperance ones.

—And, of course, we all signed The Pledge in a ceremony at which our parents, or more often, our mothers alone were present. I signed at the age of five and I remember the difficulty I had with the pen as I had only used a pencil before that. It was regarded, with christening, as part of the ritual which cleansed us from original sin. Confirmation in our early teens was the complementary ritual which protected us against its reappearance, a sort of topping up of the original innoculation. But, more important, you couldn't go to the de-monster-ation unless you had signed the pledge and that rule roped in everyone.

All the Band of Hope activities were organized by stooping, serious Willie Savage who shamed even the worst behaved of us by his gentleness – and we were a pretty boisterous crowd when we got into the Temperance Hall. The functions were often chaotic because he could not 'control' us but I imagine his influence on us was more potent and lasting than it would have been had he been a tough disciplinarian.

At the other side of the village, at one of the two farms at Burtergill lived the Wilkinsons, a well-respected family who were always regarded as being a cut above the rest of the farmers. Greg Wilkinson was a churchwarden, our local historian and an amateur vet. of great repute in the upper Eden valley. Whenever one of our dogs was injured or off-colour we always went to him for *the* mixture which was so foul smelling that, it was said, it made the wretched animal either quickly recover or die in order to avoid a second dose.

Greg Wilkinson was one of the last of generations of countrymen who knew the medicinal properties of herbs long before the development of modern veterinary practice. He never needed to refer to Culpeper's *Herbal* which had a prominent place in his house, and in many other houses. Whatever the animal or the ailment he knew which plant was required, where to find it and which part to use. Some grew miles away in the valley, one in particular, Mugwort, which he used to treat sciatica, grew by the Eden, at Musgrave, a village which lay three miles to the east. But Greg could always go straight to the plant he needed, for one of the remarkable things about a remote and agriculturally stable area of this kind is that perennial plants grow in the same places for very many years – often, I believe, for centuries. There are plants growing in the Eden valley today which were there half a century ago growing in the same hedge bottom or the same copse.

The Wilkinsons had another claim to distinction which no one else in the village had – except the Lady of the Manor – their property was entailed. It had come to Greg as the oldest son of a large family and the same rule of primogeniture would eventually pass it to Billie, his son, always known as Billie-Conq, because the schoolmaster once called him William the Conqueror. This mystical, inexorable descent of the property from father to eldest son seemed to tie the family to the land and make them much more an integral part of the village than the rest of us. They were one with Mrs Wild, the Hall, the Church and the maypole. It was regarded as a very aristocratic arrangement and definitely set the Wilkinsons apart. Billie was a kind of Prince of Wales who, whatever happened would inevitably be carried forward to his destiny. In fact the entail was only two generations old having been created by an earlier and very ambitious Wilkinson – tailor turned farmer – who had wanted to establish a rural dynasty fondly believing that an entail would last for ever.

Tom Grisedale was the tenant of two farms in the village itself. He was a big, tough, slow-moving man who was the living proof that it was still just possible for a farm labourer to graduate to tenant farmer, given the right qualities and the right wife. And as in biblical times, his chances of success were proportionate to the number of his offspring – particularly sons. Tom had three strong sons and two pretty daughters, an ideal arrangement for running a farm. The members of this family, though prodigiously hard-working were only in the first generation as tenant farmers and were never regarded as well-off, but they were distinguished and respected in another way which was even more acceptable to us, they were outstanding sportsmen – at football and cricket but especially at wrestling. There were few village sports meetings in the twenties when one of the Grisedale boys did not win one of the wrestling weights. In what little leisure they had, on early summer evenings before the round of village sports began, they could be seen on the playground (the village green) or at the Sports Club, jackets and shoes off, corduroy trousers tucked into socks, practising by taking on all comers.

Most of the men in Warcop belonged to one or other of the two Reading Rooms, there was one on each side of the beck. Now there was a social peculiarity about Warcop which I have already mentioned, the part of the village which lay on the north side of the beck ('ower t'beck') was mainly Church while the south side where I lived was mainly Chapel, and the ethos of the Reading Rooms conformed to this pattern. Our Reading Room was called the Temperance Institute. It was attached to the Temperance Hall on the chapel side of the beck and had a clientele who were mainly Chapel – or farm labourers – but were not by any means all, or mainly, teetotal. Indeed the Joiners Arms next door relied on the Temperance Institute members for most of its custom.

The three Grisedale sons were leading lights in the Temperance Institute; the Wilkinsons and the Lamberts in *the* Reading Room on the church side of the beck. The Reading Room also had the patronage of Captain Tim and Captain Jim. The gentry's support was seen in the trophies of foreign parts which hung on the walls, boomerangs from Australia, assegais and shields from the Zulu wars, mementoes from long-forgotten safaris.

Neither Reading Room had the remotest connection with reading, though the Temperance Institute (as it was rather grandly called) boasted the dust-covered remnants of an old collection of 'improving' books i.e. mainly about religion or temperance. Both Reading Rooms had full-sized billiard tables and valley-wide reputations at billiards, a further irritant in our relations with Brough.

Shopkeepers

If the vicar was *sui generis* in our social structure, so was another long-established family, but for entirely different reasons. Gregsons the grocers were unique in being rich, probably the richest family in the upper valley, yet living and regarding themselves as working people. In the middle of the nineteenth century when the railways were being driven through the valley with pick and shovel the then Mrs Gregson, a hardworking provident lady, earned a great deal of money by baking mountains of bread daily for the gangs of Irish labourers employed. This was the foundation of the Gregson fortune which was nurtured and multiplied by hard work, frugal living and astute investment for three-quarters of a century.

By the 1920s the family, as well as owning the grocery shop and the adjoining meal and grain warehouse where the farmers had their oats crushed and bought their cattle food, owned about fifteen houses in the village and a number of farms in the countryside.

The shop was owned and run by Thomas, his two nephews newly returned from the war and his sister Mary Alice. She and Thomas were both unmarried and lived in near squalor in a cottage devoid of any modern amenities. They were a friendly, happy couple who got little benefit from their wealth, except the obvious joy of keeping and adding to it. Indeed their standard of living appeared to be lower than that of the tenants of their cottages.

Thomas was reputed to be a financial wizard and read the

Financial Times avidly every day. There it was, propped up against the marmalade jar on the perpetually set table every time I went to the back door after closing time. He was the wealthiest person in the village – 'He could buy and sell Mrs Wild and Mrs Chamley put together', his forthright niece, Cissie, used to say.

He was a frequent visitor to our house until my mother joined the Co-op because, she said, they would deliver the groceries each week, though I suspect that the real reason was the divi! After that, the legend went, he never called again, though we were always on friendly terms and continued to buy a good deal from his store.

Mary Alice was a village character, a blowsy, merry, laughing woman, interested in everyone – indeed down-right inquisitive, they said. She dyed her hair, though not too expertly so that it always had a number of blotches of colours and an overall irridescence like oil on water – only surpassed in brilliance by the colour of her parrot. The parrot was the pride of her life. It lived in a tall circular cage in the living room and under it there was a permanent circle of parrot seed on the floor. On fine days she put it out of doors in a position where it could see all the comings and goings outside the shop. There it commented incessantly on everything with the most ghastly squawks which could be heard throughout the village. The noise of Mary Alice's parrot, the bump, bump, bump of the water wheel making the electricity and the tortured squealing of the circular saw in the sawmill made an unearthly trio which was the sound of Warcop in the twenties.

Gregson's shop was by far the most deliciously scented place I have ever been in. It was a glorious muddle, though Thomas could always put his hand on whatever he wanted. But he stocked everything anyone could possibly want in the way of groceries from nutmegs and carroway seeds to hams and sacks of flour. The aroma was one of the great, unforgettable experiences of Warcop – a compound of freshly ground coffee, bacon, onions, paraffin and crushed oats.

Few groceries were pre-packed in those days and they had to be wrapped in white sugar paper which lay on the mahogany counter in a pile of huge square sheets. Whatever had to be wrapped, Thomas knew to within half an inch exactly how much of a sheet to tear off. If it was a small item like boiled sweets out of the huge bottles, he skilfully twisted a small piece into a conical bag and tucked in the top. He always added up the prices in pencil on the paper wrapping the cheese or the butter – a sensible system because it meant that the bill was never lost and my mother could always check the change when I got back home.

Most of the local farmers brought their rich yellow butter to Gregson's each week wrapped in a white cloth. There it was blended and salted in a hand-operated machine and made up into neat one pound blocks. It was, I think, the most delicious butter I ever tasted.

Every Saturday evening my mother made a ritual visit to the shop, even after she joined the Co-op, as did most other village women. It was one of the highlights of the week, an occasion for chat and raillery with Thomas and the other customers who all lingered long over their purchases to hear the latest gossip as well as for the serious business of making their meagre housekeeping money go as far as possible. And Thomas was always helpful with this problem, often suggesting cheaper alternatives when someone worried about the price.

Although we got a weekly supply of groceries, my mother would want something from Gregson's almost daily and, invariably, when I wanted to go out to play. But all my pleadings that I would do the job later or tomorrow fell on deaf ears and off I had to go usually with the instruction to 'Run – or else!' Which, of course, unfailingly ensured that I walked – and slowly at that. If, as often happened, I forgot an item or remembered a wrong amount, I got a verbal lashing about having a memory like a sieve. But when I had a copper or two to spend I would be there in a flash and Thomas would take enormous trouble to show me the whole range of sweets, even making suggestions about possible permutations, two of this and six of that or three of this and four of that, which was remarkably kind in view of the size of the transaction.

There are some people in one's childhood who are always remembered with warmth and a smile. Thomas and Mary Alice are so to me but another shopkeeper evokes a memory which is quite otherwise, indeed I remember him with awe, almost with fear, after all the intervening years.

Charlie Lock was a splendidly upright man, both physically and morally, who ran the Post Office in a small haberdashery shop. He was not allowed to sell groceries because the shop belonged to the Gregson family. He was not a Warcop man but had married a daughter of Robert Beetham, the Chamley's gardener. He had been a regular soldier, and no one could ever have taken him for anything else, and ran the Post Office with military precision. The trouble was we were an imprecise lot and often failed to live up to his standards.

Because of him I suffered one of the major embarrassments of my life. When I was about ten years of age, I was sent by the schoolmaster to make a phone call – the only phone in the village was in a small booth in the Post Office. I suppose my subsequent discomfiture was my own fault because I did not tell the schoolmaster or Charlie that I had never used a phone before but took on the task as though I used one all the time.

The earpiece hung on a hook and the mouthpiece stuck out from the wall. The procedure was that Charlie would get the number for you on his phone behind the counter and tinkle the phone, which you then picked up to make the call. However, when I got my tinkle, apart from the fact that I was not tall enough to get my mouth up to the mouthpiece, I couldn't make out a word the man at the other end was saying. I struggled on with increasing embarrassment until there was a resounding click in my ear and the phone went dead. He had cut me off. When I emerged crimson-faced from the booth I was met by a stream of expletives from behind the wire grille, the gist of which was that if I didn't know how to use the bleeding phone I shouldn't pretend that I did but – as an afterthought – if I waited until he had served the other customers (double embarrassment for they had heard it all) he would make the bleeding call for me.

So ended my first attempt to use the telephone and it took me some years to recover my confidence with this modern wonder. Who would have predicted that I would become Postmaster General? Certainly not Charlie Lock!

As well as Gregson's and the Post Office there were three

other shops – my father's not too successful business, another small grocer's shop run by two old ladies and, by far the most exciting of all, there was Bainbridges.

Mrs Bainbridge sold groceries but she was also the village newsagent, the source of our comics and magazines. Her shop had an inner room entered from behind the counter which, to a small child, was a wonderland of toys, paints, crayons, notebooks and a great variety of wool, ribbons, lace and all the other flummeries that our dressmaking mothers used.

My earliest comic was *Bubbles* and my close friend, Alfie Richardson, got *Comic Cuts*. Every week we waited outside Bainbridges for them to arrive from the station. By the time we got home we had read almost every word, then we swapped. I also got the *Children's Newspaper* which was much less eagerly awaited and took all weekend to read, probably because my mother firmly believed that it was good for me. There is no one quite so contrary as a nine-year-old boy!

In my early teens I became passionately absorbed in the greatest miracle of the post-war world – wireless. The very word 'wireless' was magic to me and filled me with a sense of wonder which I retain to this day. I pored over, and kept, every written word I could find about it and spent the money I got for delivering the WI fish on mysterious crystals, cats' whiskers, coils and all the other ingredients of this modern wonder. I had seven-stranded copper aerial wire strung from the chimney to a pole attached to my mother's clothes post – held aloft in shining splendour and insulated from the earth by snowy white insulators.

Imagine my excitement when in 1923 I read in the paper that a new modestly priced magazine called *Modern Wireless* was to come out. I put my order in to Mrs Bainbridge at once. Each week I waited at the shop for its arrival as I had done a few years earlier for *Bubbles*. I read it from cover to cover until it ceased publication in December 1933 and I made my first crystal, one valve and three valve sets from plans that it published.

But the greatest glory of Bainbridge's which set it apart from all the other shops was the window display at Christmas. Early each December we waited for it with a lively and growing anticipation of all the wonders that would be revealed to us any day now. No one could ever get Mrs Bainbridge to say when she was going to set out her window: she was wise enough to keep us guessing. Each day we went out of our way coming home from school to see if it had happened.

But she allowed the excitement to grow, so that when it actually did happen the entire village found one reason or another to pass by her shop within twenty-four hours of the unveiling.

The whole window was no bigger than a normal sized bay window, yet for us there was concentrated in it the whole essence of Christmas, the expectation, the coming of something new and exciting, the bringing of gifts from afar. And over it all there was a suffused pink glow from what might well have been the Star of Bethlehem but was in fact one hundred watt bulb covered with pink crêpe paper. Mrs Bainbridge, skilful shopkeeper that she was, knew quite well that many an article has been improved out of all recognition by a soft pink glow.

The overall effect on us was magical as we peered in on the dark December evenings, the circle of upward turned little faces reflecting the pink glow against the stygian blackness behind us, for there were no street lights at that time.

There were toys of the most exotic and ingenious kind, clockwork toys with their keys at the side, books, paints, dolls – and always a doll's pram – row upon row of wonders which were examined in detail from every angle in the days before Christmas. In the twenties every boy aspired to own a Meccano set; the poorest had No. oo – indeed the number of the set was a fairly accurate indicator of a family's affluence.

Having got a set the next goal to aim at was a steam engine worked by a small meths lamp. The family income could also be assessed from the type of boiler the steam engine had, upright or horizontal. Only the better-off families got the latter. I had a vertical one which, to my great sorrow, caught fire. Watching the madly revolving flywheel in its frenzied death throes with molten lead flying off dangerously in all directions was one of the saddest moments of my childhood, for I knew that my most prized and prestigious possession was almost certainly doomed and that there would be no money to replace it.

There were sixty-eight children in the village and in the two or three weeks before Christmas every one of us pinned his hopes and dreams on one article or another. There is no accounting for taste and there was no accounting for our choices. One particular toy became more desirable than anything else in the world and we went back time and time again to see if it was still there. A kind of proprietory relationship developed between each of us and our heart's desire. Alas, when Christmas came many of us, probably most of us, were disappointed. The Hornby train set, the Meccano, the steam engine or whatever it was we wanted was probably far beyond the resources of our individual Santa Claus and we had to make do with the more modest, often home-made gifts he brought. Meanwhile our dream of what might have been lingered on for a while, longer when we discovered that someone else from a house with a richer Santa Claus had got what we wanted. Still, the willingness of all of us to share our toys made the deprivation easier to bear.

Bondmen

Most of the farmers without adult sons employed one or, in the case of the bigger farms, two farm labourers. The better-off ones also had a girl to help in the farm house but never with outdoor work except haymaking and occasionally milking. There were always between twenty and forty foot-loose farm workers in the parish, of any age from fourteen upward but mainly in their late teens or early twenties. They were almost all strangers to Warcop and were hired by the half year at the Martinmas or Whitsuntide Hirings at Appleby, Kirkby Stephen or Penrith. They were paid at the end of the half year, minus the frequent 'subs' which were given throughout the period which could not be claimed as of right but depended on the good will of the farmer. They also got board and lodging in the farm house. At the end of the half year, 'term-time', they often moved on, usually to find a better 'meat shop'.

Of all the indignities suffered by farm workers before the Second World War the hirings were perhaps the greatest. They got a week's holiday and if they wanted a change of farm they turned up at one or more of the three hirings in the valley which were held on different days. There, people of both sexes, some of them no more than fourteen while others were middle-aged, stood about along the pavements in their Sunday clothes looking red-faced and ill-at-ease about the whole process. The hard looking farmers dressed in knee-breeches, trilby hats and open rain coats walked up and down slapping their thighs with their canes and eyeing everyone on offer from flat cap down to boots. If a girl was wanted, the farmers were accompanied by their equally tough-looking wives. It was like the preliminaries to a slave market in the southern states of America a century previously.

When a farmer decided he liked the look of a boy or a girl – and the sole criterion was how much work he could extract from them – an approach was made and upwards of twenty minutes of merciless questioning and haggling followed. The practice of feeling arm and leg muscles had stopped by the end of the war but in all other respects the hirings continued unchanged throughout the twenties and well into the thirties. If an agreement was reached on a figure, the farmer placed a sum known as 'earl's money', a shilling, later a florin, in the hand of the man or girl and that was regarded as the sealing of an irrevocable contract between them for the next six months. The man or girl now became a bonded employee.

The hirings were also attended by shopkeepers from the surrounding villages, like my father, who had given credit to farm workers during the previous half year. It was remarkable how easily a man who owed us for a new suit or a pair of boots could disappear without trace during the hirings, so anyone who was owed money had to be at all three hirings by the first train and remain there until he got his man. Unfortunately, when he did so, the whole of the man's wages for the half year – or what he had left to draw – were not infrequently already gone.

So we had a sub-culture of tough, cheeky young people always among us. In view of the hours they had to work and pay which today would be regarded as derisory, the wonder of it was that they were such a robust, cheerful lot, clear-eyed with shining red faces and large red hands. Their sexual exploits were a major topic of conversation in the Reading Rooms and the two pubs. Many of them clearly had IQs which today would have carried them to the university and made them dentists or lawyers. They were almost the last of the 'mute inglorious Miltons' about whom Gray had written a century earlier. Looking back, it has always seemed a great mystery to me why a community which set scrimping and saving above most virtues should have been willing to accept uncritically a system which was so appallingly wasteful of human intelligence.

On the whole the farm workers kept themselves to themselves, though we got to know a few who stayed on for more than one term. Indeed, occasionally, one of them married a village girl – sometimes the farmer's daughter. They came to the village dances and stood in noisy groups around the door, only the ones who were 'serious' about some girl or other venturing on to the floor.

They all had bicycles or motor bikes. To own a motor bike was the pinnacle of achievement. A reasonable second-hand A.J.S. or B.S.A. cost about £15 which was a term's wages for a boy in his late teens, and acquiring one involved strict economy and often the mortgaging of the next three or four terms which the crafty farmers were always willing to allow a good boy or man to do in order to tie him to the farm. Every weekend their motor bikes could be heard roaring along the narrow high-hedged lanes – often with a girl behind who had to be impressed by quite terrifying speeds and impossible angles at corners. Many a farm boy and farmer's son came to grief on the roads of the Eden valley in the twenties. Some met tragically early and painful deaths, others serious injuries. But nothing deterred them, most of them had been too young to go to the war and so the love of risk and danger which is inherent in youth came out in their dare-devilry on the roads.

The farm workers at Warcop, and their predecessors as far back as anyone could remember had a special institution of their very own (and it really was an institution) known as 'The Big Bridge', because it happened on the bigger of the two bridges over the beck. Every Saturday and Sunday night, summer and winter, they converged on it from every corner of the parish, even from the outlying hamlets of Sandford and Bleatarn. They either sat on its high flat-topped sandstone wall or sat on their bicycles and leant against it. They were often joined by one or two village boys, though our mothers threatened us with goodness-knows-what if they heard of us being at The Big Bridge. They were quite certain that neither the language nor what was being talked about would do us any good at all – and they were right. The two staples of talk were

74

their bosses and sex, with pauses to comment on whoever had the misfortune to pass over the bridge. Most people who went to church from the chapel side of the village or to chapel from the church side, had the choice of running the gauntlet or picking their way along a muddy path through the fields. The banter about people passing was crude but always good-natured and, where appropriate as it often was, had strong sexual overtones. They rarely knew the people concerned but they weighed them up with remarkable perception from their looks, how they walked and their clothes. The same boys would have been tongue-tied if they had met them alone. But in the group they were articulate and spot-on with their comments – if a little ribald.

Late on summer evenings there used to be a rival gathering on the Coronation Seat on the green between the two bridges. This attracted more village boys and a few farm boys who wanted to fraternize with us as well as some farm girls and maids from one or other of the big houses after dinner. ('Fancy having dinner in the evening', we said.)

This group lacked the boisterous spirit of the Big Bridge. It was quieter and more gossipy. It was a place where a boy could get to know a girl in whom he was interested and the opportunities to do this elsewhere were very few.

The two Reading Rooms had little attraction for the farm men though some did join the one associated with the Temperance Hall. Their wages were so low that the pubs could not offer much of a haven. But neither the pubs nor the Reading Rooms were available to the farm girls. Youth clubs had not been heard of in Warcop in the twenties and it would have been impossible for them to join the Guides because of their unlimited hours of work, anyhow that was kids' stuff! There were perhaps a dozen or fifteen dances a year within a radius of three or four miles, so the chances of a farm boy getting to know a girl or vice versa were not high. That was why the Coronation Seat served a purpose which would surely have had the approval of Edward VII whose coronation it commemorated.

Why the twice weekly Big Bridge had always happened, even after the hirings when there was often an almost complete change in the farm labour force, was not hard to understand.

Most of the farm workers were still adolescents, though their language and physical development made this difficult to believe. They had had to leave school and home at the age of fourteen. The work was hard and long and they missed their mothers, though they would rather have died than admitted it. The Big Bridge gave them company, security, approbation and a kind of affection — all basic social needs in any age.

Characters

No two houses in Warcop were alike – at least until three pairs of semis were built in the late twenties – and no two people remotely resembled each other, indeed it was part of the way of life to cultivate eccentricity from early middle age onwards. We were a village of unique characters.

In Sandford, one of the two hamlets in the parish, there was one lady who stands out over the years in my memory, Daisy Crosby. Daisy lived alone in an utterly chaotic and far from clean cottage which, apart from the basic bed, chair and table, contained little else except a great many books and a valuable piano. She was half mad, but in the most attractive possible way. She was, in fact, a delightful, highly cultured woman, an LRAM no less, who, it was said, had 'had her head turned by too much study' – a terrible example which every schoolboy quoted when his mother got at him about his homework. She was off-balance, 'a bit queer', they said before that word was misappropriated for another purpose. But her charming smile, her intelligent if unworldly interest in everything around her assured her of a place in everybody's affections. Though the younger boys teased her outrageously, she took it all in good part. She was a child of nature, utterly absorbed in the roseate world of her music, her books and her love of the countryside. She loaned me a number of books but had a somewhat unrealistic view of what authors were suitable for a ten-year-old boy.

Three doors away from us on Main Street lived a very

different, very tough old lady called Mary Metcalfe (though no-one ever dreamt of calling her Mary) the widow of a much-respected station-master. I could never decide whether she was really a woman of iron will or whether she deliberately cultivated her severity in order to hide a warm heart. Anyhow, she always appeared to be stern and unbending. Her widowhood was clearly modelled on the Victorian pattern and I believe she saw herself as a rural vision of the widow of Windsor. Her clothes were always black – black from head to foot.

Church-going was the major joy, probably the only joy, in her life and she never missed the morning service or evensong in summer. Her deep alto voice could always be heard above the rest, which was quite remarkable for a septuagenarian in a fair-sized congregation where everybody sang. She was also a competent organist and the funereal droning of her organ could often be heard outside her house.

But under her forbidding exterior there was a sad, lonely old woman. Every evening she came to our house, sat herself plumb in front of the fire and stared into the flames for the next half-hour, her six inch front door key clasped firmly in her hands. Her conversation, which was sporadic and punc-tuated by long periods of silence, consisted in the main of mono-syllables or astringent comments on the latest village happenings, about which she was always well informed – indeed she was regarded as 'inquisitive'. I suppose she came for company. Human beings were a change from the sad memor-abilia which crowded her house.

Described in these terms she appears to have been singularly unattractive, but, oddly enough, we all held her in high esteem. 'She's a disagreeable old thing but straight as a die,' my mother used to say.

She had no financial worries with 'money in the North Eastern Railway', which, at that time, still paid dividends, but her grief at the death of her husband as well as of an adult son who was a gifted artist, did not recede with the years. Time did not heal in her case. It only increased the hurt, the loneliness, the desolation. One felt she was waiting, almost eagerly, for death to reunite her with her lost ones and, indeed, ultimately she could wait no longer and tried to take her own life.

Determined to the last, she tried to do herself in first with a hammer and, when that failed, with the carving knife. They took her to the Infirmary but she never returned, for the will to live separated from her husband and son had gone. To this day I have her two pink lustres which she left to my mother, to remind me of a staunch and faithful, if formidable, lady whose sad later life injected something quite deep and fundamental into my view of humanity. I had often stared at her silent figure, with the firelight caught in her old eyes and etching the lines in her forehead more deeply, and wondered what was going on inside her mind. She was strong and hard and sad and proud, a character quite unlike anyone else I knew, someone to be treated with respect, compassion, a little fear and a little love – a strange combination.

A few doors further along the street there was Jack Withers, the landlord at the Joiners' Arms who gave me my first dog and who, until the mid-twenties, owned a Victoria which my mother used to hire when she visited friends in Brough, where there was no station. The sheer breath-taking splendour of driving with her the three miles along the Main Road has never been surpassed for me by any ministerial car in which I have subsequently travelled.

But there was a less attractive side to the jovial, Victoria-driving, dog-loving Jack. Occasionally, indeed often, he consumed too much of his own beer and then, unlike other heavy drinkers in the village he became unmanageable and sometimes violent. Next morning he was always contrite, apologetic to whoever he had belaboured the night before and firmly resolved never to 'touch another drop'. This resolution lasted a few weeks then he broke out again. He was Jekyll and Hyde, kindly and generous when sober but, when in his cups, a raging tornado to be avoided if possible, though sometimes there was no avoiding him. On one occasion he landed himself in the Police Court and received a heavy fine for dragging a lady along the street by her hair. In the middle of another night he filled me with terror by kicking at our front door and, quite wrongly, alleging that my father owed him for some carting he had done.

But for me the warm-hearted, friendly man who gave me

my little brown dog, Peter, when I was ill was the real Jack Withers. The violence which sometimes took possession of him was the demon 'strong drink', which I knew about from the Band of Hope magic lantern shows.

At the end of the street lived the village poacher or, more correctly, a friendly, gentle old man with a little dog who was believed to be our most accomplished poacher. He was never caught in the act or seen with his haul which, we believed, was always hidden under his voluminous rain-coat.

But poaching was not regarded as in anyway reprehensible, indeed on the whole it was condoned. Of course there were no large estates and no gamekeepers within miles of Warcop and the farmers did not greatly object if someone lifted one of their rabbits. There was a river warden, the 'water watcher', living in the village but he turned a blind eye on all the vast amount of trout grappling that went on throughout the summer months in the beck. But Jimmy was not a fisherman and he was too old to grapple trout. It was said he specialized in rabbits, but also that he would knock off the occasional roosting pheasant in the depths of winter or take a wild duck from the beck on special occasions. For some reason which no-one understood the Chamleys at Warcop House claimed to own all the wild duck which nested in the willows along the beck – and they were plentiful, though always rather fewer after Christmas.

Ned Burrow was the village cobbler and I used to sit for hours in his workshop on wet days watching and marvelling at the speed and deftness with which he soled and heeled the boots and shoes and caulkered the clogs of the entire community except for the families of the handy and provident few such as Willie James. Willie was one of our two signalmen who, as well as doing his own shoe repairing, produced his own goat's milk and all his vegetables. He also augmented his wages by weaving willow shopping baskets and swills which were used to carry the washed and dripping wet clothes to the garden to be pegged on the line.

Most of the farm workers and nearly all the children wore clogs with wooden soles and iron caulkers, the replacing of which was a major part of Ned's trade. The word caulker was probably derived from the 'caulk' – the pointed piece on a horse-shoe.

My conversation with Ned was virtually one-sided for he was as deaf as a post. His unending flow of interesting conversation was punctuated by the occasional nod, shake of the head or mouthed word by me or, as a last resort, a word or a sentence written on his slate with a squeaky slate pencil.

As a schoolboy in the eighteen seventies he had memorized a prodigious amount of poetry all of which he retained. He knew every word of long narrative poems such as 'King Robert of Sicily', 'The Lady of the Lake' and 'Hiawatha' as well as dozens of shorter poems of which 'Lord Ullin's Daughter', 'La Belle Dame sans Merci', 'The Forsaken Merman', and 'The Sands of Dee' were firm favourites. He also knew endless long extracts from Shakespeare. He would regale us, a group of small boys, for two hours or more with his repertoire. I was enthralled by him and infected by the joy his poetry gave him. My own almost obsessive love of poetry was not acquired in the classrooms but from the deaf old cobbler of Warcop. And how permanent are the associations of childhood. Whenever I hear any of the old, well loved favourites I see Ned Burrow's sensitive face creasing into smiles, his last between his knees, knocking little wooden pegs into the nail holes of clog soles.

There was another gentleman who opened a whole new world for me by loaning me books. (There were not many of them in Warcop, outside the Hall where there was a large and well-filled library from which I was never at any time invited to borrow a book and the Vicarage). Though almost every house had some books, they were mainly mere accumulations of prizes presented to successive generations at the annual Sunday school anniversary when every child received a book. We were not a village of reading people. I suppose we at my home had as many as most non-gentry families. My sister had become a teacher and had acquired a good many of which John Richard Green's not too accurate *History of England* was one that absorbed me during many years of my childhood.

But Walter Wilson, a portly retired businessman, an in-comer, who lived in a cottage with his housekeeper had a huge well-filled bookcase. When they saw that I was interested they allowed me to borrow freely. Indeed, I think they were flattered that a small village boy should show such uninhibited admiration for anyone who had had the wisdom and good fortune to accumulate such a collection – a *fabulous* collection, as it seemed to me. *Adam Bede, The Mill on the Floss, Ivanhoe, The Black Arrow* – they were all there, all the old favourites. Walter Wilson's books, read not as a task but as a privilege, did much to lay the foundations of my literary taste. Clearly this fact gave him as much pleasure as it did me, and I shall always be grateful to him.

In the early twenties the smithy, a busy and important place in a farming community, was owned by a remarkable man called Jack Allonby. Remarkable because he was the good-living man par excellence in those parts, indeed he was regarded by most people, especially my father who thought him marvellous, as a kind of rural saint. Of course he was chapel, church didn't have saints anymore. He appeared to be completely without sin – or even guile. But, as always, some dissented from this view and said he was sanctimonious, though this was the worst they could say. He was a middle-aged bachelor with a sprightly, springing gait, living with his spinster sister – perhaps that was something, the knowing ones said.

No doubt they said he was sanctimonious because, being a pillar of the chapel and a local preacher, he kept all the Wesleyan rules of life which still held chapel people in bondage at that time – no bad language, cards, dancing, betting or gambling of any kind; no Sunday newspapers, work on Sundays or intoxicating liquor; Chapel twice on Sunday and Christian Endeavour on Wednesday. The non-conformists were ultra-conformists so far as their own rules were concerned. But he was not bigoted and never condemned those who fell short of his exacting standards, i.e. most of the people of the village.

On one occasion I saw him have an unconscious gypsy, who was covered with mud and blood after a drunken brawl, carried into his house when no-one else from the little crowd which had gathered would touch him. Whenever I hear of the Good Samaritan I think of Jack Allonby and his succour of that gypsy.

He allowed us children free access to the smithy. Indeed, we wandered in and out of the smithy, the sawmill, the watermill which made the electricity, the two joiners' shops and the cobbler's as we wished, stayed as long as we wished and were even allowed to use some of the tools to make things — particularly at the joiners. We were one indivisible community and, in a sense, the children were the children of the whole community.

In the smithy I was always amazed at the docility of the huge Clydesdales when they were being shod, and the whole shoeing process amazed me. Jack simply stood with his back to the horse's leg, lifted its foot by the tuft of hair and anchored it between his knees — his leather apron being split up the middle to allow for this. He then pared and hammered, in what appeared to me to be the most abandoned way, without the slightest protest from the horse. But by far the most awe-inspiring part of the process for me was the moment when the red-hot shoe, held in long tongs, was pressed on to the hoof with the acrid smoke spurting out from the sides, a smell I always liked. When he was satisfied that the shoe was an exact match for the hoof he would plunge the shoe into the small water tank beneath the forge to cool it and then nail it to the hoof, cutting off the points of the nails which came through the sloping sides.

The fascination which horse-shoeing had for me was, I think, because something made of iron which I knew to be hard and intractable, heated until no human being dare approach it closely, let alone touch it, was being attached to the foot of a magnificent living animal — and with nails at that, which always made me think of the crucifixion. I always found it difficult to believe Jack when he assured me that the horse could not feel it.

The nails used in horse-shoeing were the standard, essential tool of every village boy at conker times. No-one would have dreamt of piercing a horse-chestnut with an ordinary nail. It had to be one from the smithy and Jack saw that we were all supplied — occasionally remembering that a boy had been given one last year and telling him to look after it this time. The sharp point which could pierce the horse's hoof easily went through the toughest conker (and we had our time-honoured secret methods of toughening them) and the sharp edges and tapered point enabled it to be used to bore the initial hole to any desired size.

He catered for our needs in another way – with bowlies. After conker time was over and Christmas toys had lost their appeal, towards the end of January came marble time and after that was over, by the end of February, it was bowly time. A bowly was a hoop about 24 or 30 inches in diameter made from quarter-inch soft iron.

Jack made these for us at a small charge but new ones were not often needed as they were indestructible. They were handed down from older brothers to younger ones, sometimes from one generation to the next, and of course were bartered for other toys. Having little pocket money we were keen barterers. Bowlies were propelled around the village at great speed and with considerable adroitness by pieces of wood with a groove near the end into which the metal fitted but the better off boys had a special metal tool made at the smithy with the end bent to take the bowly. Some boys had to be content with a bicycle wheel rim as a bowly but everyone managed to get one of some kind.

Besides the shoeing the other spectacular process at the smithy was the hooping of cart wheels. The high farm carts, including the wheels, were made with consummate skill in the joiners' shops but the wheels had to be taken to the smithy to have the hoops fitted. There was a huge circular disc of steel fixed to the ground, slightly bigger than a cart wheel with a hole in the centre to take the hub. The whole huge hoop was by some miracle heated in the tiny forge – one would have thought that one side would have cooled while the other was being heated. It was then carried out by Jack and his assistant, Jim Hodgson, with huge tongs, and burnt on to the wooden wheel in much the same way as the shoe to the horse's hoof.

What a useful place the smithy was, not only to the farmers – because there were no 'agricultural engineers' then – but to the whole community. The disposable society was still in the future and when an article broke it had to be mended. If it was made of metal it was always: 'Take it to Jack Allonby', and, with enormous patience and skill he usually managed to prolong its useful life.

But, alas, in middle age saintly Jack became a non-conformist in fact as well as in name. He got an urge which was to prove his undoing. An innocent enough urge but a quite unheard of one for a pillar of the chapel and a local preacher – he got an obsessive urge to travel faster and further than his bicycle would carry him.

First of all he bought a contraption called an autowheel – the forerunner of all the auxiliary bicycle engines which appeared in the forties. It was a small engine fixed to what looked like a motorcycle wheel which was attached by a special frame to the rear of his bicycle. As it could not be put out of gear the problem was to start the engine. I can still see him running like mad down the village with his contraption as they called it and when he was almost at the point of exhaustion hearing the first whip-lash cracks from the engine. His difficulty was to gauge the moment when it had a life of its own and jump on the bicycle. If he jumped too soon it relapsed into sullen silence and the whole performance had to be repeated.

Whether the wider radius the autowheel gave him whetted his appetite or whether he tired of the troublesome thing was uncertain, but one day a brand new motor cycle appeared at the smithy. And at the weekend most of the village watched as a top-coated, mufflered, goggled Jack took off on his travels at all of ten miles an hour. Every Saturday he disappeared, we knew not where; on Sundays we knew – it was to preach somewhere on the circuit.

But it was on a Sunday that the tragedy came. Word was brought to the village that he had been found dead beside his motor bike on Orton Scar – a lonely high road on the south side of the valley. The cause of the accident was never known. His death caused a greater sense of shock than any death I remember in my childhood. This good man, the heart and centre of chapel society in the village, in whose hands the great Clydesdales were as lambs and the hard iron as malleable as clay, had been destroyed by his brief love-affair with speed. 'Older men shouldn't get mixed up with such new-fangled things,' said the women to the men who thought it had a double meaning but were not quite sure what it was.

He had a spectacular funeral. It was as though our own Pope or Great High Priest had passed on. My father said, with a sad shake of his head, that his like would not be seen again, but I didn't understand how he could possibly know that.

But we were not a village of saints – just the reverse. There was, for example, Mr Crowther who lived at Sandford. This on-the-whole amiable gentleman was a retired businessman with a private income who with his wife, son and daughter had come to live among us. He was a prodigious drinker who, unfortunately drank just too much, never being blind drunk but almost every day mid-way between total incoherence and coherence, between physical stability and instability.

He did most of his drinking in Warcop which was two miles from his home and he travelled everywhere in a horse and trap. Almost nightly he could be seen driving with demonic fury along the country lanes – a squat, hunched, figure with a white imperial beard, wrapped up in a thick coat and perched on top of his trap swaying alarmingly from side to side. Yet he never fell off, no matter how drunk he was. If he could get up on to his driving seat he could always drive – but only just. I cannot recollect a more eerie, indeed Dracula-like sight than old Mr Crowther galloping home beneath the dark trees in the blackness of a rural night with only the yellow dots of his flickering oil lamps to comply with the law – for they served no other purpose as the horse knew the way home.

The village streets were playgrounds for the children before the motors came but every Warcop mother taught her children to watch out for Old Crowther's trap. The speed at which he galloped was only rivalled by that of the farmers when taking their milk to the station to catch the last train – and they always left themselves insufficient time to get there at a reasonable speed. The Main Street where we lived resembled the chariot race in *Ben Hur* every evening, summer and winter, but Mr Crowther, half drunk, could beat them all.

We were a village with a good deal of hard drinking in spite of all the efforts of the Band of Hope and the almost universal signing of The Pledge. As well as Mr Crowther we had two or three who habitually teetered on the brink of being blind drunk but only one of them went over the edge, as he did, almost daily. Yet, rather remarkably when strong drink was rated as one of the cardinal sins by the chapel, these hard drinkers were all held in great affection. It has often seemed to me that human failings, provided they are not too outrageous, are more attractive to most people than human rectitude – which I suppose, is why the prodigal son's brother had some cause for complaint.

At the opposite extreme from the hard drinkers was dear, sweet Mary Burton, a special friend of mine who played the rather grand pipe organ in the chapel where I sometimes used to 'blow' for her when the regular blower was away. The blower sat behind a red curtain and pumped a large wooden lever up and down to provide the wind. If I stopped for a moment the music became an agonized wailing, a whimper and then stopped.

Mary lived with her mother and a maiden aunt in one of the most comfortable cottages in the village – a cottage with the special distinction of having two parlours. The victorian parlour was still a cherished institution in Warcop – the best room, rarely used for social purposes, only occasionally for Sunday tea and, in chapel homes, always to entertain the local preacher – it was also the family museum. All the household treasures and the best pieces of furniture such as the oak court cupboard, the mahogany china cabinet, the horse-hair sofa were housed in it and lovingly cared for, as well as the best plants of which the aspidistra was the most prized. The whatnot stood in the corner with its triangular shelves covered with pieces of pottery bearing the arms of Morecambe, Blackpool, Edinburgh and other northern towns. Every woman swelled with pride when she surveyed her parlour. It was a great comfort and consolation in the poverty in which most families had to live to have one splendid haven which served no everyday utilitarian purpose.

Well, the Burtons having two such havens were greatly envied by all the women who had one – or none. One of those rooms was mainly dedicated to housing a handsome mirror-bright piano on which Mary struggled with little success to teach me to play.

Learning to play the piano is like learning Greek – there is a hump, a watershed to be surmounted then you are home and dry. Unfortunately I never got anywhere near the top of the slope. Week after week I had my hour of tuition, 'Blue Bells of Scotland', 'William Tell' and all the other excessively simplified pieces that filled the primer which had been handed down to me by my sister. The trouble was that I learnt them by heart and could romp through the lot without looking which, for a time, impressed my mother but did nothing for my musical education.

Mary was much too kind and gentle to insist that I read the music but, much as I loved her and the perpetual smell of newly baked bread in their house, my main concern was always to end the lesson as quickly as possible and go out to play. However, Mary, being strong chapel, insisted on giving sixty minutes of tuition for sixty minutes pay. In summer the agony of an hour of trying to hit the right notes with the right fingers was unbearable when I knew that my pals were tickling trout along the beck or playing cricket in the Park. An hour of one tortured, laboured note after another at three second intervals with every other note having to be repeated almost made me scream.

After three years of it even my mother, to her great disappointment, realized that she was wasting her money and released me from my weekly bondage. But how I regret my youthful lack of application today! My sister had exactly the same tuition and became a competent pianist and my mother had assumed that the same treatment would produce the same results in me. It was an age when playing the piano was a highly regarded accomplishment and, because of this, countless small boys and girls wasted a vast amount of time and money trying vainly to acquire it.

In the early twenties a young artist called Donald Wood came to Warcop and boarded for a time at Mrs Dent's, along the Main Street from us, where he rented a bedroom and the parlour. He was a Leeds man who had studied in Paris and Rome and had exhibited in galleries in London and on the continent. He had served in the war and produced many striking pictures, particularly charcoal sketches of life in France and Belgium behind the Front.

For many weeks during his first summer he was to be seen around the village sitting on his folding stool, sketching with pencil or painting with oils or water colours. Whenever he was spotted a crowd of children and old men assembled behind him and watched every stroke, commenting among themselves, often in a highly critical way and in loud whispers. But we soon discovered that neither our presence nor our comments worried him in the slightest or made him self-conscious, indeed he seemed to enjoy having an audience for he was a young man of great good humour, enthusiasm and modesty. Neither criticism nor acclaim put him off. He would chat with us as he painted and ask our views on his work.

Village scenes, which seemed to me the most unpropitious subjects for an artist, emerged on his canvases as quite beautiful pictures two of which I have to this day. Looking back, I do believe he taught us to see the village with different eyes, to see forms and colours that, before his coming, we had never noticed. To us trees had always been green, sheep white and water blue. In our paintings at school, where quite progressive, indeed almost avant-garde methods, were used in teaching art, strange new colours, purple trees, green sheep, orange water began to appear.

Donald with the curly hair, the little moustache, the mobile sensitive face and springy walk was transforming our powers of observation and our ability to record what we saw, and – more important – what we felt about what we saw.

Of course, some of the older villagers were highly, but affectionately, critical. They said he was barmy to waste paint on things like that. 'That's nowt like a coo', or 'we niver saw a ewe like that?', or, when he painted Butcher Bob with his meat cart, 'Them wheels'll niver ga roond'. None-the-less they all took a considerable interest in his work and a good deal of pride in having an artist in our community.

I was quite enthralled by him, for it was the first time I had come across anyone with a clear and unmistakable artistic gift. I tried to emulate him. I painted and drew endlessly, using pencil, charcoal, paint, anything I could lay my hands on.

89

How frustrating it was when I saw that what I produced was only a parody of Donald's pictures.

Of course I had read about great artists in Arthur Mee's *Children's Encyclopaedia* but seeing one at work, seeing a beautiful picture being created by deft strokes of a brush was different. To me it gave adult human beings who possessed such a wondrous gift a new and happier dimension. It was an antidote to the traumas I had undergone about the sawn trees, the pig, Kaiser Bill, hell-fire, the accidents and all the other clouds which had crossed my otherwise serene childhood path.

Each year Donald came to us for a longer period than the year before until eventually he decided to find a studio and stay among us more or less permanently. At this time there were two chapels in the village, one for the Wesleyan Methodists and the other, the 'top chapel', belonging to the Primitive Methodists. When this latter sect petered out in Warcop and its small congregation was absorbed by the smart Wesleyan chapel with its electric light and pitch pine seats, the top chapel was sold to Donald as a studio – for which purpose it was ideal.

He painted there for many years and produced a succession of memorable pictures among which was a huge canvas of Brough Hill Fair (see title page) and it was there that I sat at his feet on many a Saturday morning as absorbed as he was. It was there that I acquired my life-long interest in painting. I never smell newly painted pictures without a vivid recollection of the top chapel at Warcop with the light flooding in from the high windows on the stacked canvases and on the slight figure with palette and brushes working in the centre.

He was a great innovator and experimenter, constantly trying out new styles of painting, new techniques and new colours. I can still see him carefully separating the yolk of an egg from the white on a marble slab, rolling it in his hands and then mixing it into the paint he was using.

Most of his pictures had two characteristics, they almost always involved animals which he drew and painted superbly well and there was usually a light area in the centre like a spotlight on a stage which grew darker towards the wings.

But this engaging man who taught me so much and whom

I shall always remember with joy had another claim to fame in Warcop. He possessed, one of the first motors in the village, a Trojan with a canvas hood and solid rubber tyres. It was the first car I ever rode in and I can hear its noisy engine still. How thrilling it was, the wind rushing past my face as we bumped along quicker than the milk train – indeed the elation was almost unendurable. And he would always give us children a ride if we asked. It was rare to see him in his motor without a few of us squeezed in beside him. He was also no mean mechanic. Car owners had to do their own maintenance and repairs in those days. It was not until the mid-twenties that we had a motor mechanic in the village, when Jack (christened Ellerton but he hated it) Walker, son of the landlord of the Railway Inn, started a bicycle repair business which soon escalated into motor cycles and cars.

But Donald went much, much further than mere maintenance. He actually completely stripped the engine down on more than one occasion. Goodness knows why, probably to see if he could do it!

On these occasions also he had his audience round the open door of the stable he rented from Greg Wilkinson as a garage. 'A'll bet thou'll have a few bits left over, Donald', old George Capstick told him as he surveyed the floor littered with nuts, bolts, cylinders, gaskets, and a hundred and one other bits and pieces.

And when the tread of the tyres wore off he burnt new grooves with a red-hot poker. Happy, happy uncomplicated days!

Donald Wood was another bright strand in the surprisingly rich tapestry of the village which nurtured and taught me. His paintings, which many of us possess now, with pride, deserve to be more widely known; his personality lives on in all of us who came under his gentle civilizing influence.

3

The Silver Strand

THE BECK WAS THE vertebral column of Warcop. The warm red sandstone cottages with no two alike straggled along it. It turned the bumpity, lumbering mill wheels which in previous generations had ground the corn but now generated the village electricity; it watered the old flower-scented meadows; half a dozen herds of shorthorns with swishing tails drank in long silent draughts from its pools; its sleek brown trout were grappled with ancient skill to supplement the food supply; its willows provided generations of boys with whistles and fishing rods and their mothers with clothes swills; it nurtured ducks galore, both the plump domestic ones kept by us and other villagers for their blue-green eggs and the shy, secret mallard which nested among the willow herb; it carried away the effluent from the septic tanks of the big houses — for only they had W.C.s — and from the kitchen sinks of the cottages. It was also a repository for the corned beef, bean and condensed milk cans which were becoming popular (we had never heard of pollution or conservation) but because of the frequent floods a bottle or can was rarely seen in it.

Its yellow flags, marsh marigolds and meadowsweet brightened window-sills as well as graves and provided the basic material for the rushbearing crowns. In past centuries its rushes had covered the floors and lit the cottages. It teemed with life apart from ducks and trout, dark and furtive life but also bright and flashing life. The minnows and the pert little sticklebacks lived in its shallows, the red-breasted males a well-loved quarry of paddling children in summer. A jar containing three or four

94

and a lump of duck weed was a favourite placatory offering to May Wilkinson, the teacher of standards 1–3, in lieu (one hoped) of having memorized a collect or one of the more obscure parts of the church catechism.

When pursued, the ugly bewhiskered tommy loachers (stone loaches) and bullies zig-zagged erratically across the bed leaving a muddy cloud, a kind of liquid smoke-screen. But they were never caught, only teased, and *they* had no placatory powers with our teacher, indeed we soon learnt that they were counter productive in this respect.

The bright-eyed water-rats plopped into the water as we walked along the banks, to enter their holes below the surface or hide away among the red alder roots. And on summer nights at dusk the warm air was filled with the whistling of otters – even in front of the houses. They and the mallard, two of nature's most timid creatures, lived within yards of our homes.

Countless dippers and wagtails dipped and wagged on stones and banks from the village to the Eden, waiting to dart unseen into their ancestral nesting places but always making a number of false moves first to deceive us. Kingfishers skimmed through the willows to their stinking holes in the bank. It always seemed odd that our most beautiful bird should live in such a filthy nest. A glimpse of a kingfisher was like the light from one of the prisms on my mother's lustres. Sandpipers in large numbers lived along the banks of the Eden but never along the beck.

The beck was a world of its own, a living community within the village community – plants, trees, fish, birds, mammals bound together by their normally gentle, but sometimes raging, habitat. But we children were also part of the beck community too. Sticklebacks and dippers, willows and water-rats, ducks and kingfishers were part of *our* world. Wearing old sand shoes, we paddled in the public parts of the beck along the village main street but on summer days we also penetrated the green, sun-flecked willow tunnels between the village and the Eden where no adults could go, the secret world of the beck people. Those were the days before the Water Authority had decided that a beck must run in a straight line and that every willow-fringed curve must be straightened. On these expeditions we turned our breeches up on our thighs as far as they would go but always ended with the lower parts soaked. Then we would lie in the sun until they were dry before we dared go home. If we fell in completely, which we all did from time to time, we found a quiet place, took off our breeches and our shirts, wrung them out with one of us twisting each end and hammered them against a wall or fence post to get the water out. But my mother always knew by the cleanness of my knees when I had been in the beck: normally, at the end of the day, the grey shaded into near black at the centre of them. One of the unpleasant consequences of wearing short trousers was that I had to wash my knees as frequently as my face and, in particular, was never allowed to go to bed until they had been scrubbed clean. But if I came home in the evening with lily-white knees I had a good deal of explaining to do. This always struck me as being rather unfair.

Every brown, moss-covered stone had a mysterious little world beneath it scurrying away with varied methods of propulsion when it was levered over with a stick. Its lighter underside revealed snails and shrimps and myriads of tiny water creatures, sometimes even a small trout might be hiding there. The water at the concave sides of the many twists and turns ran deep and dark, under the alder and willow roots. The smaller boys avoided these mysterious, rather frightening places and stuck to the shallows, wondering how on earth they would ever have the courage to grapple trout when the time came for their initiation. Tales were handed down from one generation to another about rats and otters biting off fingers and, in the case of the deepest and darkest pool, in the Eden at Penkell, of how a boy was dragged under by some mysterious creature, never to be seen again. The ancient fears of the unseen but acutely felt were still alive among the children of Warcop in the last years before the motor car and television ended their idyll.

The village loved the beck, the glittering sight of it, the gentle sound of it when the summer heat hung in the valley. But when the floods came sweeping down from the fells, brown, frothing and irresistible with bobbing branches and the occasional dead sheep, they hated and feared it and barricaded their doors against it with sandbags, boards and turf. On wild, wet nights when the water was rising ominously the older ones remembered how Thornborrow Richardson, Butcher Bob's father, had been drowned on his way home to Row End from the Joiners' Arms in 1913 and of how others in previous generations had met similar fates. A fourteenth-century, moss-covered female effigy in the churchyard was said to be that of a medieval Lady de Warcop who had been lost in the Eden – the family of Warcop had owned the manor or been associated with it from the days of King John to the end of the sixteenth century. Mothers with toddlers feared the beck at all times, summer and winter. 'Keep away from t'beck' is graven on the hearts of all who grew up there. But of course we didn't. The village grew along the beck centuries ago because of its swift-flowing, clear water; water to drink and to grind the corn. And it had adapted itself both to the stream's moods and to its physical configuration. The children built their lives around it. It was a silver strand running through all my early years.

But there was one aspect of the beck which I hated. My mother, a provident woman, kept ducks of her own. They were an assorted cross-bred group ('flock' would be too grand a word) of between five and fifteen, depending on whether it was before or after Christmas and on whether she had reared any ducklings in the previous spring.

They were hatched from eggs – about a dozen in a sitting – purchased from a local farm and incubated by a clocker, a broody hen borrowed from a farm. After twenty-eight days cracks appeared on the eggs, and with a little help from my mother in peeling small parts of the shell the young ducks emerged, probably – at any rate in their early stages – the most engaging creatures in God's creation. They were kept in the garden in a wooden coop called the duckhull, with a wire-covered run attached. But, very soon, to the growing consternation of the foster mother, they would display an obsessive interest in the large tank of water in the run. She clearly could not understand how any offspring of hers should engage in such unchicken-like behaviour. After a few weeks they were allowed to make their way down the lane and cross the road to the beck. Some inbuilt water detection device led them straight there, followed reluctantly by the worried clocker. Immediately they reached the water they would go straight in, revelling in their newly discovered birthright. It was after this first display of her family's

97

waywardness that the 'mother' used to decide enough was enough, gradually losing interest in them and soon being sent back to the farm.

For all the years of my childhood it was one of my regular, designated jobs, which I was never allowed to evade, to bring the ducks in each evening before my supper. And how I hated those obstinate ducks! The first problem was to find them. They could be anywhere on the beck between a mile upstream, and that included the mill race, the beck from the east as well as our own beck, and the Eden which was at least half a mile downstream. In fact anywhere along a stream which was in most places overhung with willow and alder. I shouted for them, 'duck, duck, duck, duck' because I had been taught to do so but I do not believe they knew they were ducks, certainly they never made any response to all my pleas, unless it was to keep very still and quiet until I had passed.

When I did locate them I had to drive them along the beck with a long stick until I reached our house and then by some means or other persuade them – more often terrorize them – to leave the water, to walk across the road, go up the lane and enter their dark, smelly duckhull where they were locked in for the night.

It was quite the most frustrating, miserable job I have ever had to do, for ducks are singularly lacking in intelligence. I would make an advance of about twenty yards, when one duck, for no apparent reason, would suddenly make a half flying, half walking-water dash back again and, by the time I had persuaded her to rejoin the others I would find that they had dispersed in all directions. The task was complicated by the presence of groups of wild duck which our lot had to pass through on the way home. Inevitably they imagined I was also driving them and, as wild duck are very wild, a few minutes of utter chaos ensued, filled with flapping wings, splashing water and duck alarm signals. All of which ended up with my ducks nowhere to be seen. At least they had sufficient intelligence to take advantage of the chaos to make a bid for freedom.

I hated this nightly ritual, which could reduce my playing time by up to one hour, so much that I almost jumped for joy when I saw them feeding in the water near to home. Once they were safely in the duckhull I would try to count them before I slammed the door and see them looking at me with those small bright eyes — at once stupid and mysterious — as though they were saying to themselves 'we led him a dance tonight, didn't we — and tomorrow we'll do even better!' Because of my tribulations in shepherding the Warcop ducks home I have had a life-long aversion to the whole duck race. I only hope my mother is not being allowed to keep any in the Elysian fields otherwise I have no doubt I shall be roped in again to bring them home — provided, of course, I end up in the same place.

But back to the beck. After flowing through the mill field where it was not very interesting and where the water from the mill race rejoined it, it ran in front of The Fox, young Mrs Buckle's cottage, through the minnow-infested shallows under the Big Bridge and then past the Little Bridge where it was joined by Flitholme beck from the swampy fields to the east. At that point there was a large and deep deposit of sand, the sandhole, in the angle between the two becks, where every young child in the village spent countless blissful hours and days. It was our beach. From there the beck meandered slowly along the side of Main Street between the road and the line of huge beech trees which a former Chamley had planted so that he could not see the dwellings of the poor from his mansion, Warcop House. At the end of the street it entered the fields, three old meadows and a pasture, which lay between the village and the River Eden. Its serpentine course through the fields was a sheer delight to us village children. Every bend had a deep place on the inner side and a shingle bed on the other. On the bank of one curve there was a vein of blue clay which was used by generations of children for modelling. The footpath to the school and church ran along one side and the insides of the bends had been fenced off by the farmers on the other side. These enclosed semi-circles which were known to us as the duck islands, were waist deep with meadowsweet, great willowherb and bog rhubarb in summer. Here and along the bottom of the willow hedges which flanked the side of the beck, the mallard nested. Every summer I knew and watched the progress of three or four nests and the twelve or so ducklings that hatched, soon to be sadly depleted by the water-rats.

But the waterhens, mistrustful, furtive birds, always built

their nests just out of reach above the water on a piece of lodged brushwood or a low branch. Of course we collected birds' eggs (now an offence) as country boys had always done; but never more than one from a nest – so the birds prospered.

Perhaps the saddest memory from those happy, summer meadows is of that mysterious bird the corncrake which abounded there, sad because it is no longer heard, a casualty of modern farming methods. Its harsh 'creck, creck, creck' reverberated along the beck throughout the spring and early summer. I followed it for hours but only saw one nest low down in the grass, found by a farm boy. Like the cuckoo it was an accomplished ventriloquist. Legend had it that corncrakes sat on their nests so close that many of them were decapitated each year by the mowing machine. Like the otter they have now gone from the beck at Warcop, only a few remain in the Western Isles, and today's village children are the poorer for their going.

Of all the delights the beck provided for me by far the greatest was the ship – a fat old willow which indeed 'grew aslant' our beck. Its main trunk was a foot in diameter and grew out over the water almost horizontally for about three feet before turning upwards. A number of thinner branches grew vertically from the trunk and from the bank. Beneath it the water was quite deep though we could see the bottom. Over the years of early childhood Alfie Richardson, Billie Wilkinson, Geoff Burton and I spent countless happy hours on it sailing to every corner of the globe. Certain branches were the levers to control the ship, to start and stop, to steer and alter speed. The look-out was high up and from it we sighted many a pirate ship but never once were we boarded though there were quite a lot of close shaves. The bridge was actually on the bank among the great leaves of the bog rhubarb through which we cut vistas upstream and down and from which all the controls could be reached.

Our nautical make-believe was, I think, inspired by a serial on the back page of the comic *Bubbles*.

In adult life Alfie Richardson joined the Royal Navy and sailed the seven seas. I often wondered whether, perhaps unconsciously, the ship in the willow tree at Warcop influenced his choice of career, whether what we are as adults has often been wrought in us by the make-believe of childhood.

My own life-long fascination with anything electrical, first acquired at the feet of Jimmy Gardiner, a rural genius who looked after the village electricity system, is another example. He taught me an enormous amount about electricity and radio and helped me to acquire the parts for my earliest radio sets. At the age of nine or so I remember using a modelling period at school to make a complete electrical circuit for wiring a house, with plasticine wire stuck to a modelling board. Perhaps I had stumbled on the solid state principle: it said much for the teacher that she did not belabour me for not producing the statutory animal or flower. At about the same age I installed a rudimentary telephone, made from a pair of earphones, between our house and Beetham's – three doors away.

But my major childhood technological achievement was a water wheel which I made from two circles of plywood cut from an orange box with a fret-saw (it was the great age of fretwork) and half cocoa tins bolted between them with meccano bolts to catch the water. The wheel was mounted on a front wheel axle from a bicycle at the side of the beck in front of our house but the pièce de résistance was the small electric generator that it worked to light a 1·5v flashlamp bulb. It was one of the wonders of the village for a few weeks and I came to be regarded as a budding Marconi – early promise which I never fulfilled, but, at least, I became Postmaster General and later, Chairman of Cable and Wireless Ltd. The child is indeed father to the man.

Grappling for trout was one of the required skills of the male population of Warcop. In times past it had been necessary for the food it produced but by the twentieth century, though the trout were still welcomed by our mothers, it had become almost a ritualistic skill, a necessary attribute for manhood. The older boys instructed the younger ones and a young man's ability to catch trout counted in the degree of public esteem in which he was held. Whether he was a ten-in-an-afternooner or a forty-in-an-afternooner reflected directly on his masculinity, both on his own confidence in it and in the views of others about it.

When a trout is caught by hand it knows neither pain nor fear except perhaps for a split second. This was of course the age-old method of fishing before it was outlawed as unsporting and replaced by the legally endorsed method which involves piercing the mouth, tongue or throat of the fish with a steel hook, keeping it alive often for quite long periods during which it is 'played' and, finally despatching it after what must be a considerable amount of pain and fear.

Although grappling was illegal it was known to everyone including the gentry that this method of fishing was widely and successfully practised. We had a full-time 'water watcher' in the village but he always turned a blind eye. His main concerns were to see that all the rod fishermen had a licence which cost 5s. a year and to stamp out the practice of ground baiting in the Eden.

The poaching aspect was unimportant because it was only practised in the beck and none of the 'legitimate' fishermen fished there. It was too narrow and the hazards of willow and alder were so near that they could ruin valuable tackle. The farmers through whose fields the beck ran when it was not on common ground did not mind in the least.

And so at an early age I learnt and practised the art of lifting fine trout out of the water with my bare hands. I became something of an expert though I was never as good as my brother who, in an afternoon on one of the fell becks with two companions had caught sixty fish.

The boys waded in the water but the men, to whom wading was too troublesome and kids' stuff anyhow, lay on the bank. The technique was to feel slowly under the bank, which sometimes went quite a long way back, and among the tree roots in the water with both hands open and relaxed. When a trout was felt there was no mistaking it. No one who has enjoyed the thrill of it can ever forget the first time he touched a fish in the water. Quite remarkably, provided there are no sharp, jerky movements, the fish are never frightened and will allow themselves to be touched and gently moved (hence the term 'tickling' which was never used in Warcop. It was always 'grappling'). They probably regarded the white hands as pieces of debris floating past in the water. After a few moments of gentle caressing the two hands were gradually locked over the fish's back, the left hand just behind the head with the fingers down the left side and under its belly and the thumb down the other side, with the right-hand fingers and thumb down the opposite sides. When both hands were in place they were suddenly locked and the fish, gripped inescapably, was simply lifted out of the water and killed.

One of the places of unfailing fascination on the beck was the mill. It was an old stone building of two storeys with the deep, damp mill race by its side. Many years ago some previous owner of the manor had artificially diverted the stream from the beck by means of a weir about half a mile north of the village where it runs for a while parallel with the Main Road (now the A66). It was brought over the flat fields, under the railway and into the park behind the Hall where it passed into a small reservoir – the 'reservoy'. In times past this gave the Lord of the Manor absolute control of the mill. The egress from the reservoy could be controlled by a sluice gate which was lifted or lowered by inserting an iron bar into a huge threaded bolt and turning it. From here it ran alongside the place where the annual sports were held, past the smithy and, eventually, through the mill to rejoin the beck in the mill-field.

In my early years it had long fallen into disuse. The building was closed, though in good condition, and the mill wheel had disintegrated and disappeared. But, in the mid-twenties, there was great interest in rural electrification, stimulated in our case by a remarkable man, Jonathan Donald, known locally as 'the electricman' who lived in Kirkby Stephen and who advised on village schemes.

In Warcop there was a generator worked by the steam engine at the sawmill which supplied electricity to the whole of the Longstaff empire – the sawmill, joiners' shop, their house and two cottages which they owned, and – because the Longstaffs were great Methodists – the Wesleyan chapel and the Temperance Institute. But the Chamleys at Warcop House also had their house wired up. After all they had to keep up with the Lady of the Manor who had her own 100v system.

Unfortunately, to reach Warcop House, the wires from the sawmill had to cross Main Street then go over the beck and the two narrow strips of grass on either side of it. That was how our second family fell foul of our first, for, being the Lady of the Manor, Mrs Wild asserted a dubious ownership over all the waste land in the parish including the six or seven foot strip between the road and the beck and the rather wider strip between the other side of the beck and the wall of Chamley's field and she would allow nothing and no-one to detract from her manorial rights.

No sooner had Jimmy Longstaff put the cables up than she sent the excellent Willie Watt, her gardener, to cut them.

For a time there was stalemate while the village watched and wondered with bated breath. The fluted brass switches and the ornamental glass shades which had been installed in Warcop House were impotent and useless. Eventually an agreement was reached between them. From it, after a long period of frigidity shading into polite coolness, a modus vivendi emerged, but the quarrel, while it lasted, was greatly relished by the entire village.

The first step in our village electrification came when the sawmill changed hands from the Longstaffs to two young partners called Ewin and Taylor. Tommy Taylor was an electricity enthusiast and he quickly extended the system throughout the village. That was when we 'got the electric' and parted company with our oil lamps and candles. When it was switched on for the first time my father insisted on comparing the two, the brass lamp with a hole up the centre and a huge white shade which hung from a beam in the middle of the living room against the single sixty 'candle power' bulb alongside it. He had no doubt that the oil-lamp gave the better light – and it probably did! But the convenience of being able to press the brass switch on the wall to get the light was too great, and even he was won over, though at 1od. a unit we had to switch it off whenever there was no one in the room.

This steam-engine-operated system lasted until the late twenties. Then, again on the advice of the electricman, Tommy Taylor acquired the use of the old mill and a new mill wheel was ordered together with all the pulleys that were needed, big ones to little ones, to speed up the slow rotations of the wheel sufficiently for the generator. For a whole summer I almost lived at the mill while the work was going on. The huge steel castings of sections of the mill wheel were assembled on the grass outside and the oak boards which formed the troughs for the water fitted between them. The stream was cleared of anything that might impede the flow of water, the reservoy sluice gate was repaired and the mechanism greased. Eventually, the weekend arrived when the electricity was switched off and the generator and batteries had to be moved from the sawmill across the village to the mill. It was one of the most major upheavals the village could remember. It was, in fact, regarded by many as a daring experiment which probably would never work. 'It won't go fast enough', 'It'll never have the power', the young men said. And the old men weren't sure about the propriety of it all. It was putting the mill to profane use.

But the dynamo was quickly bolted down onto its new concrete bed where the old mill-stones had ground the corn for centuries. The wide belts were fitted over all the pulleys and everything was ready. All that remained was to open the sluice gate and we heard the deep lumbering noise of the mill wheel again after many years – one of the distinctive sounds of Warcop. The dynamo turned, and the dial on the black ebonite switch board showed that it was producing as many amperes as the steam engine had ever been able to coax from it. The rows of huge glass batteries in the newly floored room where the ground flour had been stored began to bubble and, next day, we had our lights on again and, miracle of miracles, working on electricity produced by our old beck. No one could understand why the price did not come down, with 'no coal to buy and the water free'. But it never did.

Still, everyone took pride in our innovation, in the adaptation of the old flour mill to the new technology. We felt we had taken a major step with one foot planted in the brave new post-war world while the other was kept firmly rooted in the past.

The beck flowed into the Eden in the glebe pasture west of the church. The confluence was a right angle about which I always had feelings which were part awe and part regret; regret at the disappearance of our gentle beck and awe at the deep silent, slow-flowing expanse of water which had completely absorbed it like a satiated snake that had downed its prey and was gliding off through the trees to look for more. The beck was clear, open, shallow; we knew and loved every stone, bank, and eddy. But the river at this point was wide, deep and murky – no one knew what mysteries lay in its hidden depths. We could only guess at them from the lazy, swirling contortions on the surface, 'whirl-pools' we called them.

The river flowed around the south side of the village. It was crossed in Warcop by an ancient sandstone bridge, one of the oldest in the county, one of the few to survive the great flood of 1822, and the only crossing for vehicles between Musgrave three miles to the east and Appleby five miles to the west. The bridge had three spans and on either side of each arch there were semi-hexagonal refuges – to use the jargon of the guidebook. These quiet recesses above the river were beloved by generations of courting couples who frequently carved their initials within a heart in the soft sandstone. This was something of an embarrassment when they returned later with a different partner and, being a fickle lot, they often did so.

From an early age I was fascinated by the river though my mother always forbade me to go near it alone. But one part of it was different. From times out of memory one of Warcop's major amenities had been the bathing place on the Eden, our lido, where every boy and girl learnt to swim, breast-stroke and dog-paddle. It was in Alan Burton's field near the bridge. The bank was lined with tall alders which, like the willows on the beck, survived until the coming of the Water Authority. There was a large area of smooth pebble shingle where the cows drank and, beyond that, a flat rock bed which went down in steps to sixty or seventy yards of good swimming water.

On warm summer evenings it was crowded with swimmers and parents with their children. Going to have a 'dook' was a summer pastime which ranked even higher than cricket and tennis. Some of the more straight-laced villagers took their evening walks along the river to see what wickedness was being perpetrated there. Undressing was a problem, but we became skilful at managing the whole process behind one towel. But for the shyer ones there was always Willie Savage's wood on the other side of the river where they could undress among the bushes. The farm men, however, were never shy. When no one was about they would often go in without a stitch on them, simply because they had nothing to wear. Of course there was always the danger of getting trapped in the water if some old lady (or young one for that matter) came and sat on the bank.

The time in my life when, more than any other time, I thought my number was up was at about the age of seven when Joe Richardson was teaching me to swim. I was standing with the water up to my middle on one of the rock ledges when he told me to 'step down and have a go'. Having complete confidence in him, I did so and immediately went in over my head. I struggled like mad, taking in huge gulps of water. I opened my eyes and was shocked and terrified to find that I was under the water. After what seemed like an hour of sheer panic, but was probably about ten seconds, he hauled me out just as I felt my lungs would burst and I was about to breathe my last. It was weeks before I would venture near the deep water again and then only when I had found an instructor who did not work on the throwing-in-at-the-deep-end theory.

When the swimming season ended and the brown leaves began to fall on the water, from about the time when the great skeins of wild geese from Siberia could be seen flying high over the valley to their wintering grounds, the river provided for two or three months a very different kind of show which attracted many people to the bridge and banks – the return of the salmon from their feeding grounds off the coast of Greenland to spawn in the river of their birth.

The great fish were there in large numbers and were often to be seen struggling in the shallows with their backs out of the water. On most days when the river was low and clear it was possible to watch a female scooping a hollow, cutting a redd, in which she would deposit her eggs. Around her, two or three male fish would wait and watch and often engage in combat with each other for the pleasure of fertilizing her eggs.

It would have been easy to take a salmon (with a gaff) during the spawning for they often had difficulty in getting back to the deep water, but no one ever did. Although poaching was looked upon with benevolence in Warcop everybody abstained in the close seasons for fish, and game, and during the non-r months for rabbits. But we had no open season for salmon – we were too far upstream for that. When the spawning season was over at Christmas they left, never to return, and we did not see the great fish again until the next generation arrived from their two thousand mile journey to fulfil their destiny under the autumn leaves of another year.

The coming of the salmon and the geese were always for us two of the most romantic episodes in our calendar. The links which

the mysterious instincts of these splendid creatures forged
between far-off lands and our own hidden valley always filled me
with wonder and greatly exercised my imagination, particularly
as one of those far-off lands, Russia, was at that time a land of
revolution, of bloodshed and terror.

Every year the Carlisle otter hounds came to Warcop, sometimes more than once because the gentry believed the otters spoilt
their fishing. I was a regular follower from a quite early age, that
is until I had my personal encounter with the otter.

The hunt used to assemble early in the morning at the Eden
bridge – the huntsman, whipper-in and a motley crowd of
perhaps twenty followers who were mainly gentry, old retired
men and school children. The hunt, which went on all day and so
involved taking sandwiches, was either downstream towards
Appleby or upstream towards Kirkby Stephen. This often
involved following the river bank for four or five miles and then,
of course, we had to get home again.

On the day when I saw the light about otter hunting the
hounds had worked the river for about three miles to the east
when the scent led them away from the Eden and up a lonely
tributary called Belah Beck. In the Eden, where the water was
often quite deep, the otter could usually escape by swimming
under water for long distances and, as the water became muddied
by the threshing about of the hounds, its under-water course
could only be followed by the bubbles which came to the surface.
But in the side becks it was much shallower and there was less
chance of making a getaway to the submerged entrance to a bolt.
Perhaps this was why the otter we were following, rather remarkably, left the beck along a deep ditch and made its way overland.
By the time the hounds discovered this it had about ten minutes
start.

As I was only about eight or nine and it was now late in the
afternoon, I was feeling pretty tired. So I decided to sit on the
bank of the stream which, at this point, was about ten yards from
a spruce wood, while the rest of the hunt went off overland in hot
pursuit.

It was while I was sitting there, resting, that a huge otter shot
out of the wood and made a bee-line for the beck. But, half-way
across it saw me and stopped in its tracks. It stood quite still for

a moment, stared at me and sniffed towards me. It was, I believe, the most beautiful creature I had ever seen but I shall always remember the fugitive, hunted look in its eyes. I did not move an eyelid and, although I had my thumb-stick and was obviously one of the crowd who had pursued it for the past two or three hours, it – by some animal intuition – must have sensed that I would not harm it. After a short pause it walked – actually walked – within six feet of me, slid down the bank into the beck and swam away at great speed upstream.

A few minutes later, when the hunt crashed through the wood I think they found it hard to believe that I had seen nothing – 'absolutely nothing, and I haven't moved from here'. My otter was not found again that day, nor, I hope, any other day. From that day to this I have felt shame that I was ever counted among the followers of an otter hunt and utter repugnance at the practice of hunting this most attractive of our wild mammals.

Apart from these visits we were not a hunting village. One of the Lake District packs of fox hounds, which – as in John Peel's day – were always followed on foot, hunted the fells from time to time but aroused little local interest. Surprisingly then, the most popular game among the village boys, called Tallyho, was derived from hunting. A typical Tallyho session ranged over the whole village – gardens, woods, roads, farm buildings – and lasted for up to two hours. It was played in winter as well as summer but involved much more skill in the dark. Two boys were foxes and were given a start which was usually the time taken to count to a hundred. The pack then decided its strategy and the hunt began. A shout of 'tallyho' from a hunter meant a sighting or a clue of some kind and attracted other hunters who stealthily approached the direction of the call from various angles, eventually, they hoped, to make a kill.

The 'tallyho' call in the darkness of a winter's night always seemed to me to be eerie but, at the same time, reassuring. When I was very young, before I was allowed to play outside on the dark nights, it was always comforting to hear it and know that a game, nothing serious or evil or dangerous but merely a game, involving older boys whom I knew, was going on inside the darkness. It reduced the menace which the dark always had for me.

When I was rather older, at about ten or eleven, I was allowed to have my own fishing rod instead of the one I had made from a hazel branch. I proudly bought it in Appleby, after a long period of saving up, 5s. for the rod and 2s. 3d. for the reel. I fished with worm when the river was brown coloured after heavy rain in the upper valley – good 'worm water'. For many hours I stood alone by the swirling, coffee-coloured stream. It was the first time in my life when I remember being quiet enough just to *think*, sometimes for two or three hours, alone among the wet bushes, puzzling over everything under the sun especially the shadowy problems which beset me from puberty to my middle teens. Like all shadows they were grotesque, distorted and exaggerated. At times they clouded everything around me. But, shadowy or not, they were as impenetrable and as turbulent as the flood-waters on which my quill float bobbed so lightly.

Looking back now I cannot decide whether or not those long periods of solitude helped me to make the transition from childhood to youth. Probably not. They almost certainly induced a habit of introspection about which I have always felt ambivalent – enjoying it yet wanting to be rid of it. But I did learn in my long fishing sessions by the Eden to glory in the special unlonely solitude of the countryside; to identify utterly with the burgeoning nature around me – the bright water, the darting swallows skimming low on the river, the otter or the rabbit on the opposite bank, the summer flowers growing up to the edge of the water, the scent of the meadowsweet, the sun, the blue sky, the great white cloud galleons floating over the valley from the lakeland fells – the whole throbbing, breathing, growing presence of nature.

The waters of Warcop, the joyous waters, the angry waters played no small part in making me. The silver strand was woven into the dreams of which I am formed.

4

The Quick and the Dead

ONE WOULD NOT EXPECT the gruesome spectacle of sudden death to be part of the experience of a little boy in a small community such as ours in the deep silence of rural England, but some strange fate decreed that I should be present – the only person present – at two incidents, when two of my friends were killed. The first was when I was very young and the second in my early teens which, although outside the period of my life covered by this book, I describe now because of the strange coincidence that I should be involved on two such sombre occasions.

In 1917 I escaped sudden death because I was rather slow in climbing over a wall but I was brought face to face with human mortality for the first time in my short life. There had been deaths of village men in the war and I had seen the occasional funeral but I did not really comprehend the meaning, the utter finality of death until on a fine summer's day the life of my best friend was extinguished before my eyes, snuffed out like the candle when my mother put me to bed.

Ernie Beetham was the grandson of Robert Beetham, the gardener to the Chamleys, and he lived with his grandparents in a cottage only three houses away from us. Attached to the cottage was a large barn with a stable below, where Mrs Chamley's white horse was kept and, adjoining their garden, was a field used by the Chamleys for grazing the horse.

The Beethams' cottage with its barn, large garden and field was a favourite playground for Ernie and me and all the other children who lived nearby, and there was the added attraction of another large, airy barn in the middle of the field. This barn was used by the Chamley family as a depository for large quantities of long discarded family detritus. Among this were hundreds of glass negatives of family photographs taken over many years — house parties, boys in boaters, little girls on ponies, shooting parties, records of the comfortable life of a family of minor gentry in the early years of the century. The place was never locked and no-one minded us amusing ourselves in this treasure house. The Beethams' place always had the pull over the more restricted premises of the rest of us.

The accident happened on a Saturday afternoon. Ernie had come to call for me and we decided to play in the barn in the field. Unfortunately the horse was there blocking our way and glowering at us over the wall with all the arrogance and hauteur of which it was capable. We decided we could not reach the barn unless we got rid of the horse but it treated with utter contempt all our efforts to shoo it away.

The admonition, one of many, of every Warcop mother to her children to 'keep away from Chamley's horse' was forgotten and we started to climb over the five foot sandstone wall. Ernie was up and over before I even got a foothold and by the time I got to the top he was running after the horse which was retreating with great reluctance and in obvious anger, neck arched, tail horizontal. I was just clambering down the other side with my back to the wall so that I could keep an eye on the monster when I heard a furious neigh, saw both rear legs come up together and heard the crack, the awful crack which I hear still and which froze me against the wall.

Indelibly etched on my memory, like the glass negatives in the barn, is an image of a little boy in jersey and short trousers curling up, it seemed quite slowly, knees up to his chest, arms over his head. Looking back, this immediate foetal position has always seemed to me to be significant. Physically I suppose no more than a reflex attempt to return to the security of the womb in the face of a mortal attack but could it be that his bodily posture reflected in that instant his return to the place from whence he had come a few brief years before?

There was a group of men standing on the Little Bridge which was just outside the gate to the field and they heard the crack of the iron-shod hoof on Ernie's skull. Mark Brown, a tall slow-moving platelayer, was one of them and he, to my great surprise, was the first to cover the hundred yards across the field. He cradled Ernie in his arms and bore him gently into the house. How small he looked, almost like a baby in the arms of the huge man. His fair hair hanging over Mark Brown's arm was the last I saw of my friend.

The whole school, dressed in Sunday clothes, went to his funeral but all I remember of it was that my shoe-lace broke on the quarter-mile walk from the church to the cemetery and that it seemed as if the whole village was there.

As well as the grief which everyone felt, the accident created something akin to terror in all our parents. There were so many dangers to their children in our idyllic village, the beck, the Eden, the saw-mill, half a dozen bulls, the new motors which were appearing — but Chamley's horse was now in a category of its own. It came to be regarded in much the same way as the local dragon in a fairy story; only, quite remarkably, no-one demanded that it should be put down. It belonged to the gentry and, therefore, had to be tolerated. One can only imagine the heart-break after this for Robert, who had loved his little grandson dearly, as he drove Mrs Chamley around the country lanes in her shining governess cart pulled by the white horse.

About ten years later I was cycling to Appleby and I saw cycling up a hill about a hundred yards ahead of me, Eddie Robson, a boy of my own age from New Hall farm, with whom I was friendly. A huge, laden lorry pulling an equally laden trailer passed me. When it reached Eddie it had been slowed down to a crawl by the steep gradient and, no doubt wanting to save himself a lot of pedalling over the remaining mile and a half into Appleby, he got hold of a tarpaulin rope but, tragically as it turned out, on the near side of the trailer. The last I saw of him alive was when he disappeared over the brow of the hill with the lorry gathering speed.

A few minutes later I breasted the hill myself and found him lying in an enormous pool of blood, his head and the upper part of his body pulverized by the wheel which had passed over him. The unfortunate driver was quite unaware of what had happened and I was alone with the mangled body of my friend. Cars were few and far between in those days. The nearest house was only a quarter of a mile away but I could not leave him though I was sure he must be dead. Scarcely knowing what I was doing, my heart going sixty to the dozen, I extricated his body from the grotesquely twisted frame of the bicycle. By some dreadful contortion one of the hand grips had penetrated his mouth and was visible through his cheek.

I straightened his body as gently as I could, loosened his shirt and tried, without hope, to find a faint heart beat. But there was nothing – only death, silence, destruction, blood. I sat on the grass verge holding his hand – in retrospect a silly thing to do.

It was fifteen minutes before a car came in sight and, by some miracle, it was a doctor's. The horror, the tragedy of it did not begin to flood in upon me until I left the scene to go to Appleby. I thought of Eddie, only a few minutes earlier cycling ahead of me – thinking no doubt of the day's school ahead of him. I thought of his parents going about their morning jobs on the farm, about his sisters whom I knew and liked. And the inexpressible sadness, the awful finality of it hit me like a sudden blow. I got off my bicycle, trembling like a leaf and was violently sick. Then I cried as I had not done since my early years. The world on that fine morning looked very grey – not the soft diffused grey of the sky or the fells but a harsh, oppressive grey, and I felt that at the heart of it all was a great well of unassuagable sorrow into which I had peered that morning.

But I soon recovered and climbed up out of the trough into the sunlight. And I suppose I did so because there was a strange and wonderful thing about our Warcop. We had an acute sense that people who had died were still part of the village community. Perhaps I had better speak only for myself – I had such a sense but I think the adults had it too.

I had, of course, been subjected to what would now be regarded as excessive religious indoctrination, on Sundays matins at 10.30, chapel at 2.30, evensong at 6.30; on weekdays religious instruction every day from 9 to 10 am including the memorizing of the whole of the church catechism, many collects and vast tracts of the authorized version. Maybe that explained my feelings about the dead. It was probably not surprising that I had no doubt whatever about the existence of a spirit world behind the world I lived and played in. The barrier of the five senses which is usually regarded as separating the two was to me much less than absolute when I was very young. I not only felt but saw and heard across the barrier, or thought I did, especially at the time of the ecstatic peaks of the great religious festivals, which meant so much to us then, or in the poignant troughs at the passing of someone I had known, such as my two friends.

Perhaps a young child really does come 'trailing clouds of glory' as Wordsworth the local poet had said a century earlier; perhaps throughout early childhood he has fleeting recollections of the place from whence he came which enable him to sense the other world about him. Or maybe this is too high-falutin' and the ghost world I thought I apprehended was nothing more than the make-believe of childhood. But whatever explanations appear plausible now, the Church triumphant was just as real to me then as the Church militant. Incomprehensible as it may seem to today's teachers, at about the age of seven or eight I knew what these theological terms meant. It was one of the stock questions asked at the annual scripture inspection, to which we learnt the answers by heart. But I always had difficulty in believing that the dead could really walk about, sit down, talk, eat and do all the other things that I could do, in the sky – especially on a cloudless day.

Our religious life was all pervasive, it was just *there*, with Christmas and Easter as the high watermarks and Ascension Day and the Feast of All Saints not far behind.

At Christmas the carol singers came around the village after the day's work was done (nothing was allowed to interfere with work in those days). Observing a time honoured concordat, the church choir came one night and the chapel choir another. They always arrived at our house, which was about half-way around the village, late on Christmas Eve and we all stood at the open door to listen. It was a merry sight, redolent of Old England, Dickens and the cheaper Christmas cards. Red faces, home-knitted mufflers, alcohol-laden breath emitted with every lusty note, all in a yellow island around the stable lamp and against the blackness of the great beeches over the beck. But when they sang 'Christ is born in Bethlehem', the heavens opened for me. The altos, the tenors and the deep bass voices of the farmers became the harmony of all eternity. When they lifted up their faces to the lamp light – and faces were mostly all we could see – and poured their hearts out in the age-old Christmas message, they were for me the shepherds of Bethlehem and, though it may only have been Greg Wilkinson's stable lamp, glory truly shone around.

After they had gone, fortified still further, if that were possible, with vintage elderberry wine, I was sent to bed. 'Quick, before Santa comes.' But no sooner had my mother taken the candle, shut the bedroom door and left me in the black darkness of my bedroom than I leaned out of bed, pulled the curtains back and looked out into the night until my eyes grew accustomed to the dark village shapes – trees, houses and mountains with the velvet, star-strewn sky overhead.

The mystery of the Incarnation which lies at the heart and centre of Christian belief – 'the Word was made flesh' – was no mystery to me then, though it is now. I felt, indeed I knew, that Christ was born and His glory filled the valley, my little world, and me. The impenetrability of the mystery has grown with the years like the weeds and the moss engulfing a once loved but long forgotten garden.

And so, each childhood Christmas, Christ was born again in Warcop and not merely in the shadowy depths of the heart or mind – I sensed His coming among the cold, bright stars, in the flickering silver of the beck, among the wild dark branches which swayed against the moon, in the night music of the carols. Nature conspired with us in the simple, uninhibited joy with which we celebrated.

Yet it always appeared to me to be illogical that His birth should come in the trough of winter, in the season of decay, or, at least of the long sleep of nature, while His death, on the other hand, came at the very time when all nature is bursting with new life and new hope, when dreams of summer are reborn. I felt that whoever had arranged these things had them the wrong way round. Perhaps that was why the more elemental aspects of nature – the sky, the moon, the beck, the trees – did indeed conspire with us in the deep, flowerless midwinter to bid Him welcome.

In Holy Week the feelings evoked were no less intense but very different. For me, a pall of gloom overhung the valley which the yellow catkins, the daffodils the cowslips along the railway, the cheerful busy-ness of the rooks in the rookery above the Hall, all the joys of spring could not dispel. There was tragedy in the spring air.

The brass cross on the church altar was veiled in black, borrowed from one of Mrs Shaw's hats. On Good Friday only essential work on the farms was done but everyone with a garden set his potatoes no matter how late or how early Easter came. The origin of this practice probably had a religious significance, down into the earth on Good Friday, but to rise again.

While the men were busy with their gardens the women and children who were 'church' went to at least part of the service, though that was never for the full three hours because the vicar could not leave his poultry so long and Easter was in the middle of the time when the incubators were producing large numbers of chickens. On Good Friday I really felt the agony, the thorns, the nails, the humiliation, 'see from His head, His hands, His feet, sorrow and love flow mingling down'. When the clock struck three I reached the emotional low point of the year, indescribably sad that the writhing, tormented body was at last still and limp and pallid. 'Consumatum est', which I learnt later when I saw a picture of Jacob Epstein's sculpture, summed it up.

But then I was equally glad to be released into the cold spring sunshine to seek the more earthy pleasures of a week's holiday from school. The stigmata is easy to understand in the light of what we know now about the inter-action of body and mind. The wonder is that I emerged physically unmarked from the mental crucifixion which I endured each year.

Two days later, with that capacity for quick and complete change of mood of which the Church is capable, and which would do justice to Covent Garden, Easter Sunday burst upon us.

'Burst' which was the word used by Tennyson in 'Robert of Sicily' is the right word. Somehow it always seemed to come as something of a surprise. The altar front was gleaming white, gone was the purple of Good Friday; the brass cross was gleaming with the radiance of gold having been specially polished for the occasion with Brasso; there were spring flowers everywhere and the parson wore a newly laundered surplice. There were none of the grubby crumpled nylon horrors one sees today.

The ladies who were well enough off to afford a new outfit each year were slightly self-conscious and uncertain about what the verdict would be on their choices. The rest re-structured and re-dyed their old hats, coats and dresses often out of all recognition. It was a gay and colourful parade as the church filled up.

And then the first glorious notes of the opening hymn: 'Christ the Lord is risen today', the end of winter, the end of death, the rebirth of hope and a vision of cricket and lying in the summer grass, of collecting birds' eggs and grappling for trout. Our triumphant rite of spring was as jubilant as Stravinsky's. As with the carols on the night before Christmas I was transported by it all, by the colour, the music, the triumph of it, out of the dark oak pews into a realm of clear sunshine where there is no death, where we and the dead are one forever. And we had our own special piece of local theology. Everyone who believed anything firmly believed that all those who had died during the previous year rose with Christ on Easter morning and that they had to wait in their graves until then. This seemed to me very arbitrary – even unfair. After all, you might have to wait 364 days or, just by being lucky (if that is the right word), only a day. It also meant that no-one dared go anywhere near the cemetery on the night before Easter. All the families of those who had been bereaved during the year turned out in black-garbed force on Easter morning and remembered their dead and wept a little for them, but they were tears of relief that the dead had, they hoped, made it at last and were now safely over on the other side breakfasting on milk and honey. What would I eat, I wondered, since I detested both?

It is a major sadness of growing older, that, with the passing of the years, I have almost lost my childhood sensitivity to the great Christian festivals, their suffering and their ecstasy, and the feeling of oneness with those who had gone before. But in our little community that 'awareness' was so real that it nurtured and sustained us and, I think now, compensated us for the cultural poverty of our lives.

Strangely we never made much of Hallowe'en apart from a few lanterns carved from the swedes which Willie Savage or Alf Ellwood were always willing to give us. But the following day, November 1st, the Feast of All Saints, was celebrated in both school and church with another glorious hymn, perhaps the grandest in the English language and one which further strengthened my childhood certainty about the oneness of the quick and the dead. The 'quick' I always thought an inappropriate word when I remembered some of the old people in the village such as Old Tommie Warwick who had weighed eighteen stones and could scarcely waddle along to Gregson's for his groceries. But that did not detract from the sheer, moving splendour of 'For all the Saints'.

Unfortunately, All Saints Day lost a good deal of its separate identity in the early 1920s because of the newly established Armistice Day eleven days later. The early Armistice Days were days of great poignancy when the village, the nation, indeed the world, remembered the lost generation. We always had a service of remembrance at the war memorial with the vicar officiating, wearing his overlong surplice and a biretta, though the latter was regarded by the low church element as a papish affectation. Mr Kirby, our ex-CQMS schoolmaster, who being an ex-soldier was on the war memorial himself, marched us there and lined us up along one side of the memorial with military precision. It was a great occasion with the gentry and most of the village folk huddled around looking very sad and shivering in the early cold. We children tried hard to look as solemn as the rest and thought about the jaunty young men who had gone off to the war with a fag in the corner of their mouths and their kitbags over their shoulders, many of them never to return. But so mixed up did All Saints and Armistice become that to this day my image of the countless host streaming towards the gates of pearl is of a column of men marching across the heavens in First World War uniforms. Oddly enough the horrifying carnage of the war made it difficult to comprehend the finality of death. There were so many that surely they couldn't have gone for ever – all of them. At those early Armistice services they seemed to be all around us and, in a sense, still part of our little community. As at Christmas and Easter the barriers between us were unreal or, at best indeterminate. I wonder now whether the adults who were present felt as I did. If my own adult insensitivity to these matters is any guide, probably not. Five decades and one World War later, when I have stood with the Cabinet at the great service in Whitehall, I have felt none of the kinship with the 'glorious hosts' I felt as a young boy at Warcop War Memorial.

Ascension Day always had a happy feel about it because as our school was a Church School we had a holiday. The vicar was not too keen on mid-week services, nor were his parishioners, and so the Ascension was celebrated on the following Sunday, always preceded by a good deal of teaching and catechizing about it in the daily scripture lesson. This was another favourite topic of the scripture inspector. Here again, another rousing hymn created for me the image of a tall, shining, white-clad Jesus taking off vertically from the top of a rocky hill in Jerusalem, with an almighty 'whoosh', like a rocket from a bottle on November 5th. Seeing a TV picture of the first space rocket's take-off from Cape Canaveral, I thought, 'Good heavens – the Ascension!' I remember trying to puzzle out how Christ would land when He got to Heaven. Surely He would come up against the underside of it and bang His head if He was not very careful! – and what was the underside – soil, rock, wood or what? In the end I had to assume that there was an entrance of some kind, probably a huge trap door like the one into the attic. This would certainly be already open for Him as they would know He was coming. Later, after a particularly outrageous piece of behaviour for which I got into serious trouble with my mother, I refined this theory by a further assumption that it would surely be closed against me if I did not mend my ways. Of such stuff is theology made!

Even after the severing of old loyalties and the ending of old ways which came with the war, religious observance remained at the centre of village life and even in the late twenties and early thirties it was still a powerful influence, generating hope and contentment but also fear and guilt. Related to this continuing attachment to church and chapel and the beliefs, feelings and attitudes it fostered, there was a lingering on of the ancient belief in ghosts and other psychic phenomena, usually laughingly though unconvincingly denied. After all, if the dead were still alive and well and flitting about among us, why shouldn't they occasionally pop through the sound barrier or the sight barrier and make themselves seen or (most feared of all) heard or felt?

Yet we had only two well-established permanent ghosts in the village. The principal one was in the Georgian house on the edge of the village above the Eden known as Eden Gate in which Garry Buckle was born. My mother always swore that she had heard the rustle of its dress – it was apparently female – on some back stairs in the 1890s and she was quite incapable of an untruth while exaggeration was to her a cardinal sin.

The other one was a ghostly black dog which appeared only at night-time along a lonely stretch of road known as Penkell above a wooded sandstone cliff on the Eden on which there were a number of religious texts carved in the soft red stone including the Lord's Prayer and the Gloria. I myself saw it on two occasions and I was scared out of my wits. We had some friends, the Robsons, the sisters of Eddie whose death I have described earlier in this chapter. They lived on a farm three miles to the west of the village. Whenever one of the two daughters came to our house she always stayed until long after dark and I, in my early teens, always had to see her home along the pitch-black, tree-fringed lanes. Normally, I would have welcomed this, for the younger of the two was my own age and I rather fancied her when – at a quite early age – I started to notice girls. But, as the only way to her home, short of a three mile detour, was along the dog-haunted Penkell it became a dreaded chore. I always took my own little dog on his lead, but on the two occasions when the black apparition streaked across the road from one hedge to the other in the beam of my flashlamp, he immediately tried to run back home, an unheard of thing for him to do. Dogs invariably take a considerable interest in their own kind, but this one was apparently not of his kind but of a kind which terrified him and me too! Of course, man that I felt myself, I could not possibly reveal my terror to Peggy Robson and it was all the greater because I knew that very soon I had to come back the same way – alone!

These were our two steady ghosts but there were also alleged to be frequent sightings near the churchyard, the Hall or along one of the dark lanes around the village, usually by one or other of the village drunks of whom we had more than our share. There were also dark and whispered tales of attempts to communicate with the departed, indeed we had one go at our house. After the oil lamp which hung from a hook in the centre of the living room had been turned down, we all sat round the small circular oak table with our hands spread out around the edge, thumb to thumb and little finger to little finger. My sister, whose brain-wave it was, then started to put the questions, the theory was that some omniscient presence on the Other Side would reply by jerking up the side of the table.

There was a problem about framing the questions, for either they had to require a numerical answer, so many jerks, or to be able to be answered by 'yes' or 'no'. In the latter case, the spirit whose attention we were trying to engage had to be told 'one jerk for yes and two jerks for no'. And it worked! We got a number of very interesting answers, so interesting that it was obvious we were involved with a most perceptive and well-informed spirit. We checked him (or it) for accuracy by asking the age of the dog. The reply was absolutely accurate. We were astounded at the ease with which we could obtain information and all kinds of possibilities began to open up, such as winning the £500 football competition in the Sunday paper.

Great was the disappointment when we discovered the reason for the ghostly accuracy – my father had his foot under one of the table feet!

Echoes of witchcraft still lingered and it was usually related to the Evil One. My mother used to place a large steel poker upright in front of the kitchen fire to keep the devil out. The rowan tree which grew in many gardens served a similar purpose. It was said to have the same effect on Satan as garlic on a vampire. No-one would ever cut down a rowan growing near his house in case Beelzebub or Old Nick (as he was rather affectionately called) sneaked in and made the house his dwelling. Once in, we understood, he was terribly difficult to dislodge.

Many village remedies based on herbs have since been proved to have had some sound medical basis but a fair amount of witchcraft and astrology was also involved in many of them both in their content and the way in which they were prepared and administered – 'the moon must be full when the bistort is picked to cure worms'. And Culpeper's *Herbal* in which many families had great faith, enjoined 'let the planet that governs the herb be angular when it is picked and dried'. But who is to say that witchcraft itself, beneath the mumbo-jumbo, did not have a good deal of scientific and psychological credibility, arrived at by centuries of painful trial and terrible error?

I suppose all this adds up to us having been a superstitious lot, but silly though it may sound now, there was the certainty in everybody's mind, or almost everybody's, that our village was a community of people and spirits. For us 'the communion of saints' was not a piece of theological jargon. The village was our home and their home. And what a comfort that view of life – and death – was, how secure and impervious to misfortune it made us. Jam in the hereafter, it may have been, but how sad that the vision of it has waned with the advance of science and technology. They, certainly, can provide jam today, but have no assurances to give about tomorrow.

5

Great Days

Peter

EACH YEAR OF MY CHILDHOOD consisted of a number of huge loops of anticipation with high points of sheer ecstasy – the great days, separated by troughs of near boredom when life seemed dull and nothing outside the common round was happening. From the depth of each trough I began to look forward with reviving spirits and increasing excitement, to the next high point. Once that was over, the memories of it had faded, and the telling of it palled, the world became drab again until the next peak appeared on the horizon. Christmas, Easter, Peter, the trip, Brough Hill, the Harvest Festival and Christmas again.

In high summer when the yellow flags and marsh marigolds glowed along the beck, when the gardens were scented with pinks and lupins and the hedges along every lane were streaked with meadow hay from passing carts, there came the happiest day of all the year – St Peter's Day, the 29th June – 'Peter'.

Although our church was named after Saint Columba, our village festival, the Rushbearing, was dedicated to St Peter, the rock on which the Church was built. It was believed to have had its origins in the annual renewal of the floor rushes in the age before flag-stones and at the end of June they are at their tall, spikey best. But we lived in modern times with smooth sandstone flagstones, a strip of coconut matting in the nave and carpet in the chancel. And so, instead of carrying rushes the girls wore crowns decorated with flowers. The crowns were made from willows in the pattern of the King's crown.

Each girl had her own which had often been handed down for two or three generations.

But Peter really started for us the night before with the preparations for the sports which were held in the park after the Rushbearing. Posts, ropes, judges' tent and all the other paraphernalia were brought from the Reading Room where they were stored from one year to another. The sports ring for the wrestling and jumping and the tent for the judges (with special chairs for the gentry) were always erected in exactly the same place. The white lines for the races need not have been marked, for the lime-based whitewash stimulated the grass to grow its own dark green lines.

We children carried forms, held posts while massive mallets drove them in, sorted out ropes and generally made ourselves useful. But all these jobs were deserted when the time came to erect the marquee – especially hired each year for the dance which ended the day. The committee men knew exactly how to erect the huge bundle of canvas and poles into a grass-floored palais de danse. It was a skill which most village boys eventually acquired so that no matter how far into the future Peter might be celebrated there would always be someone who could put up the marquee. So it was with the whole festival, indeed with village life generally. Events happened year after year without any decision that they should do so, because there was always someone, a never failing succession of people, who knew what to do and how and when to do it. It was a kind of social perpetual motion.

Summer holidays were early in the year in those days to coincide with haytime, and Peter came halfway through them so it was a period when my mother's early-to-bed rule was relaxed. In school-time when I was a young child six-thirty was the inflexible rule, but by the age of ten I had managed to put it up to eight o'clock after a great deal of persuasion based on an exhaustive comparability study of the other boys in the village. But on the day before and The Day itself I went to bed with the grown-ups as the misty mid-summer dusk was settling along the beck. This privilege completed the utter bliss of those two days. Long after the last post had been driven in, the last tent peg hammered home and the men had gone to the

Railway Inn, we boys rehearsed the gladiatorial combats that would be fought out in the ring the next day, among the heavy-weights, middle-weights, light-weights, and all-weights drawn from as far afield as West Cumberland and Durham. Wrestling was the great sport of Cumberland and Westmorland and we learned the finer points and its terminology at an early age. By the time I started school I knew the difference between a cross-buttock, and a hipe. Running and jumping were peripheral to the wrestling. The great wrestlers were household names for they competed in all the village sports where, as at ours, the prize money was attractive enough – 'Upwards of £10 Prize Money', said the thick black print on our bills. Grasmere had the biggest and most prestigious sports – including fell racing and hound trailing – and also had the added attraction of always being attended by the Yellow Earl, Hugh Cecil, fifth Earl of Lonsdale of Lowther Castle, initiator of the Lonsdale Belt. The yellow carriage, later a yellow Mercedes car, in which he arrived , was a familiar sight in Cumberland and Westmorland in the first three decades of this century. For good measure he almost invariably took a number of famous house-guests with him. But in spite of the unassailable position of Grasmere, which also had a Rushbearing ceremony, many of the villages in the valley rated high in the annual wrestling circuit. As a result, most villages produced one or two good wrestlers in each generation, usually young, muscular farmworkers whose athletic achievements could have been enormous had they had the chance to develop their potential. But of course they worked twelve hours a day and their opportunities for training were very limited.

The Day itself was our very own Bank Holiday. Everything closed down, sawmill, shops, farms – except that one or two of the more skin-flint farmers extracted a few hours work from their men but, generally, only essential work such as milking and feeding the animals was done, and it was always sunny – or so it seems half a century later! A wet Peter was unthinkable.

I was up at the earliest possible moment – as soon as I heard someone astir in the house. Even breakfast, usually a glum, unpleasant meal, was leisurely and relaxed with anticipation of the delights that lay ahead. There was talk about the wrestling

– whether Bland and Robinson would be there and whether our own John Grisedale would win the All-weights; about the Rushbearing procession and what Nellie Richardson and Mary Dent would be wearing, for it was a strictly Sunday clothes occasion.

It should be explained about our clothes that there was a rigid demarcation between Sunday clothes and weekday ones, except with the gentry who wore Sunday clothes all the time. My Sunday things, like the men's, were brushed first thing every Monday morning, carefully folded and put away in the long mahogany chest of drawers. Wardrobes were virtually unknown in Britain until the turn of the century but they took much longer to reach Warcop. Woe betide us, boys or men, if we sullied our Sunday suits in any way and a tear, or even a snag, brought down the wrath of heaven upon us. We were taking the 'mense' off them my mother would say and she would never tolerate that; after all they had to last at least the inviolable minimum of one year until they were taken for everyday. Almost all the men wore blue serge suits with narrow trousers that finished a couple of inches above their boots – 'low' shoes were avant garde and, therefore, only for the gentry. I never had a proper suit as a young boy. It was always short trousers (breeches, we called them), grey jersey and long grey stockings with coloured rings around the tops, which I could never keep up. No boy got long trousers until he reached fourteen or fifteen and then he was so self-conscious that he had to be pushed out of the house to go to church, wishing with every step that the ground would open and swallow him.

There were one or two exceptions to the 'Sunday only' rule in the village calendar and Peter was one of them. For the girls and women it was their very own Ascot. The more exotic products of the W.I. millinery sessions could be seen everywhere, the feathers and ribbons, the bows and artificial fruit gleaming in the sunshine. We were a very fashion-conscious village. This was mainly because of our famous rummage sales. The gentry used them to dispose of their cast-offs and it was a favourite pastime to keep a check on where they ended up – 'Who'd have thought that that had been Mrs Wild's blue dress', they would say pointing to a new creation which had suddenly appeared, or Miss Shorrock's green one, or any one of a variety of London originated garments. They were followed through all the metamorphoses of colour and style that they underwent at the hands of our resourceful mothers.

There was a particularly skilful dressmaker in the village at this time, a small, perky, energetic woman, Mrs Allison, who was the wife of a retired police officer. With the high quality secondhand material which was always available she made us the much envied centre of haute couture in the valley. Fortunately her years of most creative activity coincided with the daring new fashions of the twenties, particularly the above knee dresses, when I discovered for the first time that women had legs. Previously the older women had only had feet which protruded from beneath their long skirts and had moved like wound-up clockwork figures.

And so Peter was the great occasion when every girl tried to outwit the fashion sleuths among the older women. The gentry too wore startling new outfits though they were often eclipsed in magnificence by the village women in their transformed cast-offs.

The Rushbearing started at the Reading Room at 11 a.m. prompt. The band were always there in their smart uniforms, 'Brough Brass' alternating with 'Appleby Silver'. There were two banners which added a touch of splendour but they really had nothing whatever to do with the Rushbearing but had been purchased when the Reading Room committee took over the running of the festival. The excitement was almost unbearable until the first bang on the big drum signalled the official start of Peter. Then the band started up in earnest, the sound reverberating against the cottage walls in our tiny village square, the echoes from each side competing with the band itself to create the most hair-raising, barbaric sound I ever remember. It filled me with an elation which none of the splendid state ceremonies I have attended since has ever been able to evoke in me.

Band playing, banners flying, girls in white dresses wearing their crowns with all the fragrance of summer around them, followed by the boys, we snaked our way over the Big Bridge and the Little Bridge, past our house with my parents on the doorstep, up to the top end of the village and then back again and through the grounds of Warcop House, out at the other side and up the long drive to the Hall where Mrs Wild, the Lady of the Manor, waited for us in regal splendour on the sandstone steps — with enormous hat, parasol, and necklaces galore, beside her, the two ugly Pekes on which she doted, though they were universally disliked. Her housemaid, her only maid in those difficult post-war years, then served us with lemonade made from crystals, and cake.

The grounds of the Hall were always immaculate and, for Peter, at their best; lawns cut and edged, splendid topiary, memorable displays of flowers — I particularly remember a brilliant bed of salvias — and never a weed in sight. And all this was because of a quite brilliant gardener — a small, wiry man called Billie Watt. To this day I judge a garden (Kew and Wisley not excepted) by the standards achieved by this rural gardener. He was a humble but tough man who loved a pint and a crack. He was paid a pittance plus a cottage in the Hall grounds and he was, I think, a truly happy man. The source of his happiness could only have been the way in which he excelled at his work — the well-kept lawns, the clipped yews, the cleanly swept drive, the excellent vegetables he produced. Creating order and beauty from the thrusting relentless anarchy of nature, his skill and enthusiasm as a gardener were transmitted to others. We were a village of good gardeners.

Not only the Hall gardens but the cottage gardens too reached their annual peak of beauty and perfume at the time of the Rushbearing, and, here on the ancient lawn were the brightest of their treasures in the pinks and lupin-scented crowns laid on the grass while we drank our lemonade and mothers fussed over their daughters' hair and dresses.

The road from the Hall to the old sandstone church was a tunnel of translucent green in June. The confetti patches of sunlight which filtered through the leaves covered the banners, the crowns and the dresses with a glittering, many-splendoured mantle.

The band was deafening along this final stretch, but, as we approached the lych gates there was, for the children at least, a mild feeling of anti-climax. Our hour of glory behind the band was almost over, the lemonade and biscuits were behind us (or rather inside us) and immediately ahead there was a long and boring sermon in a church which would be packed to capacity. But it soon passed when we remembered the sports in the afternoon.

The girls went up to the altar in twos to deposit their crowns on the top step during the singing of 'Onward Christian Soldiers'. Each year, after the service they were hung on the wall of the south transept and filled the church with an aroma which ranged from the delight of Rushbearing day through decaying vegetation a fortnight later to a steady pot-pourri-like fragrance in the backend of the year.

Soon we were pouring out into the sunlight again – children, mothers, a few fathers and visitors who had often left the village years ago and were making their annual pilgrimage to Peter. Home across the fields as fast as our legs could carry us for our dinner.

The adult sports were held at 3 p.m. ('prompt' the bills said) and the children's sports started half an hour earlier, but these were always a bit of a bore. After all who really wanted to be organized into three-legged races, egg and spoon races and the like when there were ice-cream carts and stalls selling strawberries and a huge marquee to play in as well as wrestling to watch? But we went along with it, actually we had no choice, because the committee and our parents thought it was 'nice' to have children's sports before the adults had theirs and, therefore, assumed that we would enjoy them.

But from 3 pm ('prompt') it was sheer, unorganized delight for us. We stared wide-eyed at the mighty wrestlers, household names all of them, muscles bulging under their uniforms of black embroidered drawers and white tights (for all the world like long johns) as avidly as Roman boys might have done in the Coliseum. We gorged ourselves on ice-cream, pop and strawberries to the limit of whatever pocket money we had managed to accumulate. A regular weekly allowance was unheard of. I was seven before I really mastered the difficult skill of drinking pop from the bottle. The difficult thing was to push the glass marble up with the tip of the tongue and drink at the same time.

We wove in and out among the spectators around the ring, occasionally reporting to our parents, mainly in the hope that the general euphoria would produce a few more pennies. Then, at the height of the blissful afternoon, with all its excitement about who would be champion at the end of the day, we children followed a strange ritual. We would wander away to spend a little time in one of our secret places, in the bushes around the small reservoir, the 'reservoy' which stored the water overnight to work the water wheel next day. The same phenomenon occurred during our annual 'Christmas Tree' when a few of us would leave the Temperance Hall to play quietly in the wood-yard behind the sawmill for a little while before returning to the high jinks inside. It was a strange thing to do. Perhaps it was because the enjoyment would be all the greater after a short absence from it.

The sports did not end until the sun was dropping low in the west over the great rookery and the large oaks began to cast their shadows across the golden light which covered us all, and at the end we were all around the ring. We were always filthy after our long day and our Sunday clothes had definitely lost some of their 'mense' but the evening of St Peter produced its age-old alchemy. We were all transmuted into pure gold. The bleary face of the village drunk, the hawklike features of the Lady of the Manor, the imperial beards of the vicar and Mr Crowther, the bulging tights of the wrestlers, our grubby strawberry-smeared faces were all glowing and alight in the evening sun.

But soon the last wrestler was felled and the winner emerged triumphant. 'By God – Bland's done it again!' they said. The 'upwards of £10' was distributed in envelopes by Mrs Wild to polite applause. Then the sun was gone and we all looked mortal again and felt rather cold.

The dance came later in the evening and, from an early age we were allowed to go for a time with our parents and sat on the forms from the Reading Room which were arranged around the sides. The marquee was lighted by hurricane lamps strung on a wire between the poles. My clearest recollection is of the smell, a mixture of crushed grass, perspiration, cheap perfume and paraffin.

The younger men, mainly farm boys, crowded around the entrance end and kept up a torrent of uproarious laughter among themselves at jokes which, I noticed, our parents took some trouble to prevent our hearing. The girls sat on forms but only the ones who were 'going strong' sat with their boyfriends. It would be assumed by everybody that matrimony was a certainty when this happened.

After the two pubs had closed the number of the men and the volume of noise increased appreciably. After this also no set of the Lancers ever got through without at least one of the circles collapsing on the grass into a struggling heap of legs and arms from which girls emerged blushing and the boys laughing louder than ever.

The first time I was allowed to go I was fascinated by this outlandish behaviour of the adult world. I had no idea that the serious people I knew in the village behaved like this. Even the older women ('old' to me was, I suppose, about thirty-five) did the valeta and waltzed – how they waltzed! Some actually did the polka, always a great favourite with some of the older, more wiry men. But mainly the older women watched and noted who disappeared from the marquee and for how long – and drew their own conclusions. Many courtships, some marriages and quite a few illegitimate births were said to have started at the Peter dance. It was remarkable, in a village where many attitudes were still almost medieval, that no stigma attached to illegitimacy. Three of my best friends were without fathers. We were a small, close, isolated community with no town nearer than thirty-six miles. All our girls and boys were taught by their parents to keep themselves 'respectable' but, if they didn't no one made the slightest difference in their attitude towards them. Anyhow, there were too many to ostracize. Everybody was strong 'Church' or 'Chapel' or, like us, both, but there was no religiosity, no humbug or hypocrisy when anyone fell from the straight and narrow path. The son of a highly respected farming family who worked at a local auction mart was sent to gaol for fraud but the esteem in which he and his family were held by everyone was completely unaffected, indeed, added to it was universal sympathy and sorrow at their misfortune. This was not an amoral attitude but, I think, the natural kindness which bound the community together.

And so the Peter dance was a wild affair but an important one in our village calendar. It was the occasion when the village let its hair down – or part of it did, for the gentry and the vicar never came and this meant that their otherwise restraining influence was removed. Everybody saw the other and more human side of everybody else, one not always apparent in the church, or the pub, or the fields, or the shops. It was a night of happy abandon when we reverted to the Merry England of three or four centuries earlier. Of course the cows would have to be milked at six-thirty the next morning, but who cared while the Lancers got quicker and the grass soggier?

It all ended at one o'clock but, if Peter fell on a Saturday, it was the inflexible rule that the last waltz must end by midnight, then the National Anthem for which everyone stood to attention, even, by some miraculous manipulation of their instruments, the band. Playing around in the Lancers or outside in the dark was permissible indeed expected, but playing around with the King was absolutely taboo.

The Trip

The trough of despond after Peter was the shortest of all, for our annual outing to the seaside came in mid-July.

As we were a long way, in fact equidistant, from the North and Irish Seas we rarely went to the seaside at any other time. I cannot remember any family apart from the gentry going for a seaside holiday. If we got a holiday away from home at all, and few did, it would be to stay with an aunt in Carlisle, or Darlington, or Durham.

The schoolmaster, Mr Kirby, was a go-ahead, gay man (in the undebased sense of that word) who came from the Fylde in Lancashire and organized an annual outing for the whole school. He had remarkably progressive views on our education and made a great thing of allowing us to choose the venue by secret ballot. He believed it was a lesson on the machinery of democracy. But I always suspected that, somehow, he rigged the ballot to ensure that we chose Blackpool almost every year and Morecambe once in a while. However the democratic process was abruptly abandoned one memorable year when after a secret campaign by a new teacher, we chose Whitley Bay in the North East. He was livid with fury but, having boasted about how fortunate we were to have a free choice, he was stuck with our decision and so Whitley Bay it had to be. But big, garish Blackpool was really our favourite as well as his. Where else could we paddle in the sea and see lions and tigers as well – and, of course, his relatives lived nearby.

The trip was paid for by a series of money-raising events

during the previous six months and, in Warcop, the two favourite activities for this purpose were the Whist Drive and Dance and the Rummage Sale — both held in the school, for we had no public hall except the chapel-dominated Temperance Hall.

It is difficult now to remember the extent to which people had to provide their own entertainment in the days before television and when radio was in its earphone infancy. In the summer months everyone took walks, long walks, in the evenings and on Saturdays and Sundays. The village and its surroundings was honeycombed with footpaths along the beck and the river, through the woods, up on the high fells — ancient rights of way established by generations of walking villagers. Now alas almost all are overgrown and forgotten.

In winter there was always a great deal going on but by far the most frequent and popular event was the Whist Drive and Dance, because everybody played cards and danced, except those who were strong chapel to whom card playing was a certain road to hell. Card playing was the principal form of self-entertainment. Warcop people were prodigious card players, able to remember every card that had been played and, therefore, every one that hadn't. As a game progressed, they knew with uncanny skill the whereabouts of every unplayed card. And to revoke was the most heinous of offences — at least equivalent to attempted theft — while to trump your partner's trick labelled you as an idiot who should not be allowed to play.

The players sat at the long school desks which had been arranged in twos facing each other so as to make a wide table with a seat along each side. There were problems with the bulkier farmers and the more rheumaticky old women when the winning couples had to move after each hand, but no one minded — this was how it had always been. The prizes were donated by the gentry, the shopkeepers or the farmers — the latter being much preferred as donors as theirs usually included a fat cock chicken.

After the Whist Drive, which consisted of twenty-four hands, never more never less, the desks were pushed back to the walls, the floor was swept, making everybody sneeze, and then scattered liberally with white lux flakes. As it was made of pitch pine and had been eroded by decades of children's clogs and caretaker's scrubbing brushes till the knots and nails stuck up a quarter of an inch above the rest, it certainly needed this friction-reducing agent.

While all this was going on refreshments were served in the Infants' Room. On very special occasions a Tatie Pot Supper was provided. The tatie pots – Lancashire Hot Pots to those who do not know about these things – were made and given by the mothers, probably a dozen of them, and were kept hot on the stove and in the schoolmaster's house next door.

The music for the dancing was provided by a pianist and, occasionally, a fiddler. Some of the more prosperous, we would have said pretentious, villages with huge modern village halls (often converted ex-army huts) engaged dance bands, replete with the sweet twenties sound of saxaphones, from 'ower t'top', Darlington or Durham, but Warcop stuck to its pianist with his pile of sheet music by Francis Day. He always took the front off the piano to increase the volume. The waltzes, valetas, polkas, and lancers, as well as the new foxtrots and one-steps, went on into the early hours, sometimes interspersed with songs which were invariably the old Victorian and Edwardian ballads. Alf Jackson sang 'The Last Rose of Summer' through his waxed moustache, Jack Watt the rabbit catcher, provided he was still reasonably sober, sang 'Little Grey Home in the West' and pretty Isa Robson's speciality was 'Grandmama's First Ball', about how grandpapa asked grandmama for the second minuet. We were still Victorians at Warcop a quarter of a century after the old Queen's death, still loving, indeed wallowing in, sentimentality and nostalgia.

The outcome of the event would be that about £10 would be added to the annual Trip Fund. If the money raising was behind target and the date of the outing was looming up, Mr Kirby would slip in a rummage sale or two because they were easy to organize and never failed to produce £7 or £8, even £10 if Mrs Wild had returned from her winter stay in London. Warcop loved its rummage sales which always included a magnificent cake stall where every mother tried to outdo every other. There was also a white elephant stall which, if it could

138

by some magic have been transposed from the twenties to the eighties, would be immediately snapped up by the hoards of antique dealers who haunt every country sale today.

By one means or another sufficient money was accumulated to pay for the 'charra-bang' and for dinner and tea. Of course we saved up our pocket money at school as well. Every week our savings were entered in a blue exercise book and, by the great day, each of us had three or four shillings to our credit. I have never, since then, felt as affluent as I did when I drew out my cash the day before the trip.

For some reason which I never understood, my mother always insisted that I had a bath the night before the trip and a thorough soap-all-over one at that. The normal rule was a bath, including hair, on Friday and a good wash including legs every evening as well as a wash excluding legs in the morning. The extra tub slipped into the weekly routine certainly helped me to sleep in spite of almost unendurable excitement, but I suspect that there was a more obscure reason for it. Perhaps it was that her child was to go over the hills and far away among strangers and there must be no possibility of criticism on any score whatever; so clean clothes, shoes, nails, teeth and a bath just in case! It was a long tradition, ingrained in working-class families, that they must always be prepared for every eventuality.

When the great day came I got up at seven then, most unfairly I felt, had to be scrubbed again, in spite of the bath the night before. Breakfast was almost impossible to swallow in the excitement, especially as my mother always insisted that anyone going away must have a good one. When I was very young there was also a fair amount of apprehension as well. 'I hope he'll be all right' I heard her saying to my father, and certainly, the goodbyes to all the family, except my mother, could not have been more poignant, when I left the house, had I been emigrating to Canada.

My mother always took me to the meeting place in front of the Post Office. Children were coming from all directions with their mothers and some had had a three mile walk to get there. We had a weird assortment of school satchels and bags containing our ten-o'clocks, a mid-morning snack, with a bit extra in case we were hungry during the day.

The fifty or sixty of us all in our Sunday best, faces shining, hair plastered down with water, were almost beside ourselves with excitement when we left home, but when we came together at the meeting place, looking slightly unfamiliar to each other, the excitement was almost beyond human endurance.

I remember my first trip not long after the war. I had never been parted from my mother before and I held her hand as I jumped up and down yelling to make myself heard. Eventually, at eight o'clock a low, growling noise rose above the shouting, coming from the church road and getting louder. Immediately there was dead silence with every face watching the corner and, quite suddenly, there it was – a long, red monster, Robinson's 'charra-bang' from Appleby. It was very high off the ground with a huge canvas roof and open sides. The seats went from one side to the other with many doors and, because of this, once you were in, the only way from back to front or front to back was *over* the seats.

There was a well-established pecking order in the allocation of seats, older ones at the back and younger ones in front. The headmaster and his two assistants spread themselves out – not that that was very effective in curbing the high jinks that went on, especially on the return journey, in the near dark of the July evening. As some of the boys and girls were fairly mature fourteen-year-olds, and rural children mature early, there were a number of self-conscious liaisons between them and there was always a good deal of manoeuvering to sit near to each other.

Eventually, after endless admonitions from our parents which continued as we were clambering up into the seats and often, indeed, after we were seated, we were all safely on board and the doors at the end of each seat were slammed, the engine was cranked up. This was an operation requiring great strength but also dexterity in case it back-fired and broke an arm. Slowly we pulled away, leaving behind a group of forlorn, moist-eyed mothers who watched us until we were out of sight.

It was strange how different the village looked as we stared back at it from the charra in the state of exhilaration induced by its maximum speed of about thirty-five miles an hour. But soon the village was left behind us, and within a few miles, the countryside was no longer familiar. We were in foreign territory. Looking back now to the twenties I believe I felt as an astronaut must feel as he leaves the good, old familiar earth behind and is rushed out into the unknown.

Before long the charra was growling its way through Kirkby Stephen where we waved and shouted to surprised shopkeepers who were sweeping the fronts of their shops. Although Kirkby Stephen was little more than one long straggling street it boasted a weekly market, a cinema in the Oddfellows Hall, a girls' Grammar School and two railway stations, but its people regarded themselves as townies, very superior to the villagers who came there to shop or sell their sheep and cattle.

Up over the high eastern end of the valley we went, then down along the narrow tortuous road to Sedbergh which was completely new and strange to us – a town (it also was really a large village but it looked like a town to me), where the streets were so narrow that the charra had to crawl through them in case it scraped its sides. Lancaster, dominated by the Ashton memorial on one hill and the castle and church on the other, was our first stop in mid-morning. Here in the all-pervading stink of linoleum which was manufactured there, we ate our ten-o'clocks though most of us had been nibbling non-stop since we started. The schoolmaster had arranged for us to be shown around the castle. He was always one for 'widening our experience' as he put it – Lady Plowden would have approved of him. We had a guide who impressed me very much with tales of times past which I now know to have been highly apocryphal. Yet he fired my imagination so much that for weeks after I got home I made models of castles and organized exhibitions in the wash-house at home for which I charged an entry fee of a halfpenny.

Among other wonders, he showed us a decaying oak door which, he said, was a thousand years old. This thought gripped me so much that when he wasn't looking I picked a tiny fragment from the door, carefully wrapped it in my hanky and took it home. However, when I proudly showed it to my parents I was disappointed that they did not make quite as much of it, or of my enterprise in acquiring it, as I thought such a trophy merited.

As we drove along the dull flat road from Lancaster to the sea there was always a competition, I suppose to relieve the mounting tension as we neared our goal. Sixpence for the first to see the Tower and Big Wheel, the twin symbols of Blackpool. I never stood a chance because on the winding road with the charra constantly changing direction I was never sure where to look and, when the cry went up that somebody had won I was usually looking in the wrong direction.

Eventually a huge sign 'Welcome to Blackpool', after which we crawled for ages through endless, dingy streets to the sea-front and the sea at last! Here was the end and purpose of all our whist drives, dances and rummage sales. As we gaped at the bigness, the brightness, the openness of the promenade we knew it had all been worthwhile. As for the sea stretching out to the horizon, my first sight of it took my breath away. Water had played an important role in my early years but that was the gentle, clear water in the beck and river at Warcop. I had never imagined as much water as this. Here was a new, different, glorious world for a little boy who had scarcely ever left his small village with its mountain wall. And there was a whole day ahead, almost a life-time to a seven-year-old.

We were met by the schoolmaster's mother and brother who lived nearby, and taken to a restaurant for a meal of fish and chips, ambrosia indeed! All I remember of the restaurant, apart from the food, was that the windows were steamed up and I could not see out except by clearing little patches. But every minute there deprived me of the sea and the steamed windows stopped me seeing it, as well as the sand, the Tower Zoo, the South Shore Pleasure Beach, and all the other wonders which Mr Kirby had dangled before us when soliciting our votes for Blackpool.

I have often wondered how the three teachers avoided losing some of us. Our ages ranged from five to fourteen and we had no experience whatever of getting about in a busy town. After the meal we went off holding hands in twos and threes but, by some miracle, we all turned up, perhaps after one or two alarms, at the meeting place at the end of the day. All were in varying degrees of grubbiness and dishevelment, some with queasy tummies, all with money gone but rich in sticks of rock with 'Blackpool Rock' printed right through them, in red, tiny pottery dogs and plaster rabbits won at the South Shore and — an absolute essential — presents for our parents.

My recollections of how we spent the intervening six or seven hours are a chaotic jumble of memories, probably because there were so many things we wanted to do and, after sampling one we rushed breathlessly to another, sometimes returning to a delight we had enjoyed earlier in the day. It is difficult to say what gave us most enjoyment; it was all so strange and new and unlike anything we had experienced before. Perhaps it was the marvel of the waves dashing against our legs and making us run back to the dry sand until we got used to it; the showing off and acting as though being buffeted by the waves was an everyday experience. Even seaweed was new to us. Everybody took a piece home because, we had been told, a piece of it hanging outside the door was a reliable predictor of the weather, turning soggy if it was going to rain and hard as a board if it was to be fair.

The rather moth-eaten animals in the Zoo were a major attraction and everyone tried to be there at feeding time. But the lions and tigers were a disappointment. They wouldn't roar, they wouldn't get angry and look fierce. All they did was to snooze, occasionally opening a baleful eye to look disdainfully at us and then go off to sleep again. I had expected raging beasts like the one that attacked David Livingstone in Darkest Africa but these were like weary old pussies — indeed for all the world like our old ginger cat at home. And the monkeys obviously were lousy and spent the whole time picking fleas off each other. Belonging as we did to a farming community where people cared for their animals almost as well as they did for their children, where we were used to appraising animals, it came as something of a disappointment, if not a shock, to see how decrepit and sad caged animals could be. But we loved the fish in the aquarium. The great bass swimming straight towards us and only half an inch away behind the glass were bigger than any fish we had seen, except perhaps the spawning salmon in the shallows of the Eden in the backend of the year. Some of the knowing ones said that the glass magnified them and that they weren't half as big as they looked. But they seemed fit and well and enjoying their captivity. We knew about fish and felt more at home among them than among the exotic animals.

Everybody went all the way to the South Shore. 'Go by tram', Mr Kirby had told us but the garish attractions of the Golden Mile were too great and so everyone walked, sampling shrimps, candy floss and all the other delicacies that were on offer on the way. The problem about the Pleasure Beach was the, to us, exorbitant cost of every pleasure. The big dipper, the helter-skelter, the hoop-la, the coconut stalls, everything cost the earth and, by the time we had passed along the Golden Mile, our cash was getting low anyhow. Coming from Warcop we had virtually no experience of having to pay in money for our enjoyment – though we often paid in other ways! At home our pleasures were self-made or pleasures of the countryside free for the taking. But here everything we wanted to do, every one of the thrills available to us, had to be paid for and each one we sampled not only whetted our appetite for more but also reduced our capacity to *pay* for more. It was a new, sobering, bitter-sweet experience. How we wished we were rich enough to try everything.

At the end of our perfect day when we gathered at the meeting place we were very tired, sated with food and pleasure, regretful that it was almost over, but – if we dared to admit it – rather looking forward to getting home where we could boast about the places we had been and the things we had seen. Anticipation of this trip, the event itself and the recounting afterwards (with suitable embellishments) all gave me almost equal pleasure. We were used to sharing; it was an important part of our lives which would have been much poorer without it, and the recalling of pleasurable events was just that, an attempt to share with our families an experience we had enjoyed.

We were a quiet little group, subdued by physical exhaustion, as the charra crawled through the streets towards the green fields. But the comfort of the seats as well as the thought of home, combined with the warmth of the camaraderie of all being together again, soon revived us and, by the time we reached Kirkby Lonsdale, we were very much alive and had to shout at each other to make the telling of our exploits heard. Here we stopped outside a pub, to relieve ourselves the schoolmaster said, but long after that process had been completed the teachers were still inside the pub. They usually emerged when we started to sing 'Why are we waiting', looking very jolly and smelling of something that slightly resembled my mother's best elderberry wine.

By the time we got to Sedbergh the darkness was beginning to fall and this was a new experience, to be out in the dark without my mother, in a comfortable charra and far from home. By now we were singing at the top of our voices and in those days we had an enormous repertoire of country ballads which we had learned by heart at school: 'Early one morning', 'Barbara Allen', 'Drink to me only', 'Clementine', 'Ten Green Bottles', 'Loch Lomond', 'Annie Laurie', 'Widecombe Fair' and many others. The Jacobite songs were special favourites which was rather remarkable as we lived near enough to the border for some of the ancient distrust of the Scots to linger on among us.

As it grew darker the older boys and girls – no longer fearing detection or, if caught, reprimand, because of the general euphoria affecting the teachers as much as us – started to use the illicit versions we had for most of the songs. They were, at worst, mildly rude but never obscene. In the main they were highly irreverent of authority, especially that of the teachers and such local personages as the Lady of the Manor. They often substituted names of known people for the names in the songs. All pretty tame by today's practices but extremely daring in the twenties. The teachers wisely became completely deaf on these occasions.

And, of course, the older pupils who had crushes on each other had contrived to sit together in the back seats. The term 'petting' had not been appropriated by the activity it describes today. In the twenties petting was what mothers did to their children, not what teenagers do to each other. But what went on in the back of our charra certainly would not qualify for that description today. All of it would be regarded as unutterably tame by the same age group in the seventies. Holding hands, a fair amount of whispering, for the bolder ones a lightning peck on the cheek, often as a dare, and nothing more. Yet to the ones who did it, and to the younger ones who watched, it seemed very grown-up, very naughty-twentyish.

At about ten o'clock we would begin to recognize familiar silhouette shapes among the dark hedges and hills which glided past us. We knew every tree, every farm building, every land mark around our village. We saw the coloured lights on the railway signals at Musgrave Station though the milk train had gone two hours ago and we knew when the road took a left-angled turn over the railway bridge that we had only two miles to go. A mile outside Warcop there is a short little hill known as the Stoupes; from the top of this hill it is possible with skill to free-wheel all the way into the village on a bicycle. When we reached the top of the Stoupes in the charra we felt that we were starting on a grand entry into the village. The crowd of waiting parents in front of the Post Office always knew by the noise when we had reached this point, but when we came into view around the corner from Row End farm there was no melody left, nothing but shouting, bawling, at the top of our voices with an occasional 'hip, hip, hurrah' discernible among the chaos.

We were back. Out we filed, sixty-three little boys and girls – even the older ones looked little now – into the pool of yellow light in front of the charra, dirty, hoarse, arms filled with rock, seaweed and all the mementoes of our day at the seaside, unrecognizable as the scrubbed and tidy lot who had left in the morning. After a great deal of weaving in and out of the crowd I found my mother and, my hand in hers, started for home through the darkness and the long, long task of describing every detail of the day – well almost every one – and some which perhaps did not quite happen but which seemed necessary to establish beyond any doubt the uniqueness of our remarkable day.

Brough Hill

When the nights were drawing in and the cold winds were beginning to blow down from the eastern end of the valley, when the fells had lost the benignity of summer and started to glower at the villages below, when even the most idle farmer had cut his oats and stacked the sheaves to wait for his turn with the travelling thresher, when the apples were ripe and the swallows had gone, we had our second great village festival, Brough Hill Fair.

Now Brough was, we thought, a rather barbarous village three miles along the Main Road to the east at the foot of the Stainmore Pass and they claimed Brough Hill as their fair too, though it was clearly, unmistakably in Warcop parish, astride the Main Road on a bleak hill called Brough Hill. Because of the incontrovertible evidence of the parish boundaries which, in those days, we all knew — 'The Township of Warcop' — the stone beyond the fairground said, we resented their claim and regretted having one of the oldest horsefairs in the kingdom on an inappropriately named place. But it had been held there for centuries and, as with much in rural England, nothing could change it.

It just came round on the 30th of September, as it had always done as surely as Peter or Christmas Day. It had a momentum of its own. A week before, the farmer who owned the long, narrow field which skirted the road removed the fence, otherwise he would have lost it. A squad of strange police were drafted in to a small circular police hut which remained there permanently. We had no policeman in Warcop. By mid-September horse-drawn caravans began to converge on us from every direction, occupying any wide roadside verge or piece of wasteland they could find, for the farmer kept them off the fairground as long as he could without endangering his fencing — or, indeed, his person. The Lady of the Manor claimed all the wasteland and verges in the parish and took it very badly if the gypsies arrived too soon and were too obvious around the village, but so did everyone else for there was a love-hate relationship with them. We were certainly proud that they had travelled so far to our fair but we also feared them not a little. This, I suppose, was partly the ancient villagers' fear of the stranger who comes among them, partly because of their, on the whole undeserved, reputation for thieving and partly because of the unprepossessing looks of some of them. Whatever the truth, everything movable was locked up at night around Brough Hill time — especially poultry.

Swarthily beautiful women dressed in gaudy clothes and wearing huge ear-rings began to visit the houses selling clothes-pegs and willow baskets. If they came to the back door my father always said they were 'after something'. Sometimes they offered to tell your fortune, provided 'you cross my palm with silver' which, I imagined, was a mystic gypsy formula but soon learned meant a minimum of 3d. (and not much of a fortune for that!).

At the same time flat carts, traps, and single horses were seen in increasing numbers tethered outside the pubs most afternoons and evenings and in large numbers at turning-out time. Then, the first fights occurred on the grass between the Railway Inn and the smithy, with no holds barred, fists, knees, boots, heads, the lot, even the occasional knife. Wild looking long-haired horsemen galloped bare-back about the village roads and washed their horses in the beck.

We called them all 'potters'. Many were genuine Romanies, some were horse-traders who took to the road in the summer months and some were travelling folk who preferred the open road to the anchorage of a house. The travellers eked out a living by collecting scrap metal, old clothes or anything else they could lay their hands on and selling simple, but often faulty wares, mainly seconds which they had bought wholesale in the towns of Lancashire and Yorkshire. As most of the country roads did not see a motor from one week to another, it wasn't a bad life – apart from the rather outrageous harassment they suffered.

They all had large families. Insecurity invariably increases the fertility rate. The potter children were bright-eyed, and sharp as a needle, though few of them could read or write. I stared in envy at these children as I walked along the rows of caravans with my mother to see the sights in the evening before the fair. They did not have to go to school; they did not have that abomination, a Sunday suit, to worry about. My mother puzzled over where they all slept and, in the caravans, which were no more than a flat cart covered with a tarpaulin, how they kept their bedding and clothes dry. Damp in any shape or form in clothes, bed or walls, was one of my mother's greatest fears. 'It's a wonder they don't catch their death of cold', she would say. It was part of the inherited lore of country people that damp could kill and, of course, consumption, which they believed to be caused by damp was still the greatest killer. Streptomycin and all the other wonder drugs still lay many years in the future.

By the time the great day arrived there would probably be two hundred caravans with twice as many horses crowded into the lower part of the fair ground. The vans, all horse-drawn, ranged from the simple covered carts to purpose-built ones of elaborate design which were decorated with bright colours and traditional Romany motifs. They were a sheer joy to see and, as so many were used for fortune-telling our mothers made it their business to see inside them and emerged with a catalogue of their contents – 'Crown Derby, silver, silks and satins' they said – often, I suspect, exaggerating to emphasize the strangeness and the foreigness of the potters. 'Aye, I wonder how they came by that lot', the husbands would say.

Their powers of clairvoyance were believed to be uncanny. The village women would recall how Gypsy Rose Lee had told them things years ago that had come true – two deaths within the year, a dark man from over water, a long journey, etc. But they all had their palms read so often and were, therefore, told so many things that it would have amounted to a breakdown in the law of chance if some of them had not come true.

Every year the Earl of Lonsdale arrived from Lowther in one of his yellow Mercedes cars to meet the gypsies most of whom he knew by name. The tall, rather stooping figure with side-burns and a kindly face, dressed in tweeds with knee breeches and spats, went along the rows of vans followed by a crowd of sightseers, calling on family after family, cracking jokes and exchanging reminiscences. He had spent a year of his youth with a touring circus. I still have a price card from a box of toffees which he autographed for me. 'Good luck to you, Lonsdale', he wrote.

'Lordy' as he was known to everyone in the two counties, was born in 1857. His escapades as a young man shocked the Victorians, and, as a not-so-young man the Edwardians as well. But by the twenties he had become one of the best-loved though most flamboyant figures in Britain, particularly in sporting circles where he was regarded as the supreme national arbiter of fair play. He was, if anybody ever was, a legend in his own lifetime.

From 1882 when he succeeded his brother as fifth Earl, he enjoyed an enormous income from the family coal and iron mines in Cumberland. Firmly believing that he was the last of the Earls of Lonsdale – he had no children – he spent the lot, refusing to plough any of it back into his extensive estate. While other landed proprietors were improving their estates and diversifying their sources of income he demanded that everything should go towards maintaining him in the style to which he had long been accustomed. His life was a continuous battle with his trustees to extract from them every last penny to maintain him in his regal, indeed more than regal, way of life at his castle at Lowther, eighteen miles west of Warcop, at his magnificent hunting lodge in Rutland and at his great house in Carlton House Terrace. He had over fifty indoor servants at Lowther alone, as well as an army of gardeners, grooms, keepers and estate workers.

My parents were friendly with one of the men who worked in his sawmill and my mother often took me to stay with him and his family in their cottage in the village of Askham where everything was owned by Lordy and everyone employed by him.

By the early 1920s, because of his incurable prodigality, his refusal over the preceding decades to plough anything back into his farms and his utter inability to change his life-style in the post-war world, he was in considerable financial difficulties. 'I am broke', he wrote to a friend. But after the General Strike most of his income from the mines dried up and his problems became insoluble. We know all this now but, at the time, apart from the sale of his hunting lodge, Barleythorpe, few signs of strain were visible.

No matter what the problems, Lordy's golden image was maintained as bright and burnished as ever. He was never seen without his huge cigar and his white gardenia; his yellow cars were as immaculate and as numerous as ever and he handed out half-crowns, £1 notes and £5 notes to anyone who rendered him the slightest service as he had always done. It was said that he gave away £5,000 a year.

He was not only the grandest rural potentate in the Eden Valley but the grandest in the land, outdoing, often at prodigious expense, his rival Lord Derby in Lancashire – even outdoing Edward, Prince of Wales in his amorous adventures. (And that was saying something!) He was a hangover from another age, feudal but also generous in the extreme. Even the Cumbrian miners who slaved for poor wages in the pits below the sea, loved him, his sportsmanship, his showmanship, his good humour, his flair. His like will never – can never – be seen again.

Our own village gentry, it seemed to me, were minnows in the scheme of things compared with the yellow Earl. At a very early age it was only too obvious to me that social gradations depended largely on possessions and that those with great possessions demanded, and were accorded, esteem according to their possessions. But, I began to ask myself, did they deserve the special standing we gave them? Did they really deserve to be known as 'the toffs' as many people called them?

Looking back, it seemed that the weather at Brough Hill was always the opposite of the Peter weather. It was invariably cold and windy, but Brough Hill would have lost a good deal of its wild, back-end quality without the Brough Hill weather, a term which was used throughout the year. It went with the flying manes and tails of the horses as they were galloped along the crowded road, with the blue smoke streaming from the chimneys of the caravans and the boilers of the refreshment tents, with the ham and tongue teas.

The crowd, unlike that at Peter, was mainly composed of strangers who disgorged from charra-bangs and horse-drawn brakes early in the day. The locals were swamped by people who spoke with strange accents. Farm workers came in from miles around and parked their bicycles in Harry Dent's yard in the village at 6d. for the day. Joe Dent, his son, was said to have bought his new BSA motor-bike with the proceeds one year.

The main activity of the day, indeed the original purpose of the fair, was selling horses along the road where the Roman legions had marched almost two thousand years earlier. Many of them had been brought down in droves from the high fells and were almost wild, but each one had to be caught and haltered by its purchaser. Much of the excitement of Brough Hill was in watching the mighty struggles between the stallions and the hard men who fought to subdue them. To me the scene had a heroic, epic quality as the conflict between man and nature was fought out to the inevitable end when hands were slapped to seal the bargain, money passed and the proud animals submitted to their fetters which they would never again lose.

Donald Wood, our artist, laboured for years to capture and record the scene, the wild, rearing horses herded together by the crowd, afraid but determined to resist, the cloth-capped grim-visaged men who were equally determined to master them, the turmoil, the noise, the urgency – 'Sell the bugger and scram' was the golden rule the potters followed. Each year Donald spent the whole day from dawn to dusk sketching the horses, the men and the caravans. Eventually he assembled them on a huge canvas (see frontispiece). It was his masterpiece on which he worked for years of my early childhood while I sat at his feet in his studio. It is a remarkable picture, warmly praised by Queen Mary at an exhibition of his work in Bond

Street, in 1922. Saddeningly evocative for those of us who knew Brough Hill half a century ago, it recaptures the last wild fling of the age of the horse.

Many horses changed hands after showing their paces along the road, an examination of their teeth, and prolonged haggling. But every year even the shrewdest judges of horseflesh were taken in, almost always by the gypsies who would strike camp and be far away among the maze of by-roads in the valley by the time the animal's shortcomings came to light. A great deal of Brough Hill was, in fact, a battle of wits between the smart boys who knew all the tricks of the trade and the locals who thought they did but didn't.

And the travelling people were not all horse traders. There were the Cheap Jacks selling silk stockings and china tea services with a ten-shilling note thrown in. Of course, it had been borrowed from the bemused purchaser who had become utterly confused by the salesman's stream of sales talk and the pressing, excited crowd to the point where she really believed she was getting a tea service and a ten-shilling note for five shillings. But the sharpest of all were the con men with their small, green, beige-covered tables which folded for a quick getaway. Many a half crown was lost by farmers, who usually could afford to lose them, by the three-card trick. 'A could a sworn the bluddy thing was under that'n' – but it never was.

The noise seemed to us to be deafening, but we had no experience of crowds. Brough Hill was the first crowd I was ever in. The strident, urgent shouting of the Cheap Jacks, the con men and the genuine traders who were trying to extract the maximum amount of cash from the crowd in the few hours available, the frantic neighing of frightened horses, the laughing, the swearing were all, like the weather, part of the rather barbarous quality of Brough Hill. The smell of it was unforgettable – crushed grass, wood fires, ripe fruit, wet clothes and boiled ham in an all-pervading stench of horse manure.

In 1920 I spent 6d. of my Brough Hill pocket money at one of the stalls, on a hard back book of animals. It was the very first book I chose and bought myself and, with my Queen Victoria, became one of my most treasured possessions. I have it still, though unfortunately Queen Victoria disappeared somewhere down the years.

The potters, the weather, the noise, the smells were the Brough Hill that I knew and loved, but there was another aspect of it which gave it cosiness and conviviality – the refreshment tents, those oases in the uproar which dispensed ham and beef teas from mid-morning until early evening. My parents ran one to help out their precarious income from the shop. The tent was a house-like structure with tarpaulin roof and canvas sides which was kept rolled up in our warehouse for the other 364 days of the year. We also had a huge portable boiler heated by a coal fire for the water. The trestle tables and forms were borrowed from the Temperance Hall. For days before the 30th of September my mother cooked huge hams in the wash boiler and roasted sides of beef in the black, brass-knobbed oven by the side of the kitchen fire. She baked bread and cakes and scone and buns until the house was bulging with food and filled with the most delicious smells I ever remember. Everything had to be taken to the fair ground early in the morning, the tent having been put up the night before.

The chalked notice outside said 'Ham and Beef Teas, 1/6'. My mother's reputation as a cook kept our tent filled all day or until the food ran out. The burly, big-handed men wearing their flat caps and overcoats, crowded on to the forms which looked too small for them, with the shiny-faced country women who turned up their noses at the townies who ventured in. My mother and one or two helpers served the meals. My father's function was to stoke the fire and take the money but he never divulged exactly how much he had taken.

My pals and I used to push our way among the crowds, trying to look at every new wonder as though we saw this kind of thing every day.

It was all very different from Peter which was an intimate local affair at midsummer in the sheltered park of the Hall. Brough Hill was open both to the weather and to all comers. It had a strange and exhilarating vitality of its own which those who experienced it before the horse was replaced by the internal combustion engine can never forget.

Unlike Peter, there was no dance at the end of the day. A

marquee would probably have blown down and, unlike most of the villages in the valley, we had no village hall. 'If only we had built one instead of that silly war memorial', they said. The Temperance Hall was controlled by trustees who regarded dancing and drinking as devilish activities. But our go-ahead satellite hamlet of Sandford had a brand new wooden village hall complete with stage, supper room and all mod cons and they held a 'Grand Dance' every Brough Hill night to compete with the bigger function in the very posh, brick-built, maple-floored, Memorial Hall at Brough.

All the Warcop folk walked or cycled the two miles to Sandford rather than give any support to the preposterous claim of Brough that it was their fair. But the children were not allowed to go. Two miles along a dark, wet country lane over the haunted Penkell was more than the most easy-going mother in the village would allow her children to endure. All our entreaties as we grew older were of no avail, 'You're not going and that's that.'

And so parents and young children ended Brough Hill day around their fire-side with, maybe, a walk out to see the goings-on in the village particularly outside the Railway Inn.

A few days later the last caravan disappeared into the distance, the litter was cleared, the farmer's fence went up again and the strange policemen returned to their beats. Our brief contact with the exciting world beyond the valley was over for another year.

Harvest

Nothing can ever equal the joy of harvest time in the days before the farm horse was replaced by the tractor, at least for those of us who lived in the villages. The farmer and his farm workers struggling against the weather probably took a different view. In Warcop the deadline for getting in the hay was St Peter's Day and for the oats, Brough Hill Fair, but only the well-organized farmers and those who could – or would – afford additional labour finished by then.

Opposite our house, beyond the beck and the beech trees, there was a small meadow in front of Warcop House belonging to the Chamleys but let to a farmer. On a day in late June I would be awakened very early one morning by the mowing machine and for the next fortnight the street and the houses would be heavy with the sweet, nostalgic smell of hay. June was dominated by hay. It was everywhere. The roads and roadside hedges were bedraggled with it and it was a major topic of conversation.

Most of the farmers were only too glad of the help of the schoolchildren, for most of the hay-making was done by hand with the wooden hay-rakes produced at Longstaff's sawmill and the dangerous looking two-pronged hay-forks. The school closed for the summer holidays in the middle of June so that we could help. From the age of about eight I delighted in helping any farmer who would have me. The rake was almost twice as big as I was, but I soon learnt to manipulate it with a fair speed though at the cost of many blisters on my hands.

Most farmers carried out five processes on the neat rows of cut grass left by the mowing machine. First it was allowed to dry for a few days – maybe one day, maybe a week depending on the amount of sunshine – then it was turned with the hayrake and left for a further few days. It was then strowed (scattered) and, after another drying period, was raked into ridges. If it was reasonably dry every few yards of each ridge was then raked into a haycock. The final stage, the timing of which, like that of all the others, depended on the weather, was to fork the cocks into a number of pikes. Most of the hay, being inside a pike, was now protected from the weather and the farmer could start another field and, eventually have all his hay ready to lead away to his barn or to a large stack.

I got no pay for my efforts. The farmers were too stingy for that. Anyhow they knew that many boys would help whether they were paid or not and so they didn't pay us. But there was a compensation, the farmers' wives always made provision for us in the enormous meals they brought to the fields and the sheer joy of sitting on the hay with the farm workers eating home-made meat pies and apple pies and drinking tepid tea out of the lid of a milk-can was all the reward I ever wanted. And not being paid had another advantage, we could come and go as we pleased. My mother generally approved of my helping with the hay because, she said, I kept clean in the hayfield, but I was always strictly admonished that I must not use a hayfork and I must never, never lead the horses. The first of these rules I had no wish to break but I am afraid I was often in breach of the second.

The farmers always seemed to believe that a farm-worker was wasting his time leading a cart load of hay to the farm which could be up to half a mile away. 'It doesn't tek a man ter do that,' they said. And so, rather remarkably, they were always willing to entrust a huge load of hay pulled by a giant of a Clydesdale to a young schoolboy. I have never accepted the popular view that the horse is the most intelligent animal – the dog is – but I do believe that the farm horses at Warcop knew they could take advantage of a small boy. And there were many difficult moments when a horse would stop with its dangerously backward-tilting load in the middle of a hill and refuse to go another inch. The drill in this case was to back it into the hedge obliquely across the road and wait for somebody to come who could assert his will over that of the horse.

On one occasion the horse refused to go into the stackyard where the hay was stored but turned off into the main farmyard where it made a bee-line for its stable. Unfortunately the door was open and I ended up with the horse inside and me, as well as the load of hay, on the outside. But, miraculously, although a great deal of the hay was led home by boys, there were no accidents – only frights, many frights which would have driven our mothers frantic had they known. Occasionally they did find out, as the more spectacular horse-boy incidents became common knowledge through talk in the Reading Rooms or pubs or, most often of all, on the Big Bridge.

The corn harvest did not need the help of us schoolboys. The binder – pulled by one, sometimes two, horses and driven by one man – cut the oats (we only had oats at Warcop) and, by a miracle of technology, tied them complete with neat knot into sheaves which it then spewed out on to the ground. Another man followed and arranged every six sheaves into a stook, three twos propped against each other pyramid fashion. Two or three men could do the lot.

But the corn-cutting provided all the boys of the village, and some who were no longer boys, with high excitement because of the rabbits and rats. The binder went around the field in decreasing circles (or oblongs). As the area remaining uncut grew smaller and smaller all the animals hiding there were concentrated into a rapidly disappearing refuge, surrounded by a growing area of bare stubble where there was no cover. Eventually, when the cutting was almost completed, they had to make a run for it but, as the remaining corn was now surrounded by boys and men with an assortment of clubs, usually fencing posts, few escaped to the hedge. No dogs were allowed because of the danger from the blades of the binder.

In retrospect, it was a cruel business. I could not be dragged to participate in it today but, I suppose, in some respects we were an unfeeling community as far as animals were concerned, except in the case of domestic pets. A farming community cannot afford to be emotional about animals and we had no sentimental feelings about rabbits which, in those days before myxamatosis, were a considerable pest but much sought after as food (they sold at 1s. 6d. a couple). Upwards of twenty rabbits were quite often bagged in one field of oats and the farmers, except the meaner ones, always shared them among us. As for the rat, it was the most hated animal of all, believed to be the carrier of disease, and killed at every opportunity.

A few weeks after the corn had been stacked at the farm the itinerant threshing machine, drawn by a huge steam engine with all its brasswork gleaming, would appear one evening and be hauled into position alongside the stack. The wide leather belt was put in place over the engine flywheel and around a smaller pulley on the side of the thresher. The whole of the next day the chugging of the engine could be heard throughout the village and a column of black coal smoke was shunted upwards from its chimney with every chug.

The sheaves, after having been cut were fed into a huge mouth at the top of the thresher and the grain came out of a narrow chute at the side into jute sacks which were then carried away to a (hopefully) rat-proof granary. The straw oozed out of the back and was stacked as winter bedding for cattle, not wastefully burned as today. In addition to oats and straw the thresher also emitted chaff for which there was no longer much use although the hens got endless pleasure foraging among it for the occasional ears of corn. In the past it had been widely used for filling beds and there were many chaff beds still in use in the village — the chaff being renewed at threshing time. Straw was still used for filling though it was much less comfortable than chaff, but the most sought after beds were filled with feathers, saved by housewives over many years until they had sufficient for their mattresses. The sheer, glorious luxury of a feather bed cannot be described, it had to be experienced.

Here too, as in the harvest fields, there were rats galore which, with the enthusiastic help of an army of small boys and a miscellaneous collection of dogs, were destroyed in large numbers.

June was dominated by haytime and September by the corn-harvest. October was the month of harvest festivals, genuine, rollicking thanksgivings that all was safely gathered in and that our survival and the survival of our animals in the coming winter was assured. There were four of these festivals in the parish, in church, chapel and in the chapels of the two hamlets. Many people went to all of them.

The church festival was a pretty tame affair, in fact nothing more than the ordinary matins and evensong plus the harvest hymns, an abundance of michaelmas daisies around the altar, a few swedes on the chancel steps and a sheaf of corn in front of the pulpit. The vicar thought the enthusiastic celebrations at the chapel rather vulgar and kept his in a low key.

But his parishoners disagreed. They looked forward eagerly to the three Wesleyan harvest festivals and, when they came, savoured them with uninhibited joy. The service at Warcop chapel, a handsome building erected in 1872 and the pride of the circuit, was held on a weekday, usually a Monday evening. The nights were colder and the huge coke stove was lit for the first time. Its heat made the nearest seats give off a delightful smell of warm pine which mingled with the scent of phlox and fresh vegetables. All the electric lights in their sparkling glass shades were turned on – the church could only boast its antiquated liquid gas lighting system. The whole building was warm, bright and cosy. In front of the elaborate pitch-pine pulpit there was a great mass of autumn flowers and vegetables covering and spreading beyond the Lord's table as the Methodists called it. The modern pipe organ was played by Mary Burton, my music teacher, as the congregation filled the steeply tiered seats to capacity, everyone bending forward hand over face to pray for a moment on taking their seats. No one kneeled in chapel – that was a church practice.

The Methodist minister was invited to preach but, if he was not available, and his diary must have been full of harvest festivals at this time of the year, one of the better known local preachers came. The sermon lasted for anything from thirty minutes to forty-five and the pattern of it was always predictable – twenty-five or so examples of the wonders of nature all leading inexorably to the conclusion that there was a pattern, a design, a plan behind them all which could only be the work of Almighty God.

The old well-loved harvest hymns were sung with the kind of lusty enthusiasm that only Methodists can achieve. The volume of sound, the harmonization of the voices, the sheer gusto of it made everybody feel better, safer, more at one with each other. 'Sheer emotion', said the vicar when told how marvellous the chapel service had been.

After the service we all went along the road to the Temperance Hall where the chapel ladies had prepared a ham and tongue supper. It was always ham and tongue. The long trestle tables were covered with spotlessly white table cloths and we all stood among them to sing grace. They were great singers, the Methodists. One of the clearest recollections of my earliest childhood was standing there, my face level with the table top, between my parents while the doxology, a verse from the Old Hundredth, was sung without accompaniment. The deep, unbelievably deep bass voices of the farmers in the small hall impressed on my memory an image of intense masculinity, an almost frightening, primitive maleness.

Meanwhile the produce was brought from the chapel and arranged on the stage. After supper Greg Wilkinson, farmer, animal doctor, local historian, auctioneer and devout church goer into the bargain, sold it all by auction, enlivening the proceedings with his comments on both the things he was selling and the people who were bidding for them.

We got home very late and very happy with a bag of assorted cabbages, swedes, beetroot, carrots or whatever my mother had managed to buy without paying too much.

The hamlets of Bleatarn and Sandford both had small Wesleyan chapels — in the case of Bleatarn the 'tin chapel' made of corrugated iron. At both the pattern and the atmosphere were the same as at Warcop except that the supper and sale had to be held in the chapel. This meant that there was a chaotic interval after the service during which most of us stood outside in the starry night until the supper tables were arranged.

It is not easy now to recapture the fervour, the good fellowship and the sheer enjoyment of those simple thanksgivings. They differed from many of our religious observances which, one felt, were often ritualistic incantations, not very different from my childhood ritual of walking backwards over the Little Bridge. The chapel harvest festivals were a simple, uncomplicated expression of thanks, joy, relief. And when they sang the grace in the Temperance Hall they really meant it.

All creatures that on earth do dwell,
Sing to the Lord with cheerful voice

6

Dogs

A HUMAN LIFE CAN be chaptered in many ways – by years, by decades, by clearly demarcated periods – infancy, youth, college, army, etc. But one of the ways I like to sub-divide my life is into the lives of my dogs, the lovely dogs I have owned, or more often, that have owned me, and given me a life-time of affection, devotion and amusement. Since my early childhood I have scarcely ever been without a dog as a companion and friend.

I suppose my present attitude to dogs has developed since I got Peter at the age of four, but even at that early age I remember loving him dearly and getting great comfort from him, especially from the feel of him. On one occasion my mother boxed my ears for falling into the beck, a fairly regular occurrence (the ears and the beck!) and, as always, I consoled myself by sitting inside my toy cupboard which was in the thickness of the wall and about thirty inches high and using the backs of his silky ears to wipe my eyes – which he uncomplainingly endured though he must have hated it.

The relationship between my dogs and me has always been like that, never master and servant, never cringing submission before a superior being. I have always tried to allow my dogs to keep their dignity which is a first requirement for a happy dog. The most rewarding relationships with dogs are those which recognize and respect the dogginess of the dog and the humanness of the human. My dogs have never had their spirit broken. They have always been allowed in the end to assert their independence rather than be made to cower defeated and humiliated in a corner. Sometimes this has meant a bared fang and a snarl of defiance, sometimes a minor bite for that is a dog's nature, his last defence, and when he cannot resort to his last defence his character becomes an emaciated shadow of what it should be. But when this has happened, for example in the middle of a severe reprimand, or a physical chastisement with a rolled up newspaper it has invariably been followed by unmistakable signs of contrition, a cold nose pushed quietly into my hand or a quiet sidling up to lean against my leg – rather heavily in case I did not notice. And, if that failed to attract my attention to the obvious apology, there would be a rather awkward clambering exercise to lie sprawled over my feet, stealing sly glances up at my face. When any of these attempts at reconciliation were made, all it needed to release a deluge of affection, of tailwagging and invitations to go out and forget about it all, was one kind word from me. The greatest punishment for any of my dogs was to be ignored, for overt affection to be withheld. But when normal relations were restored the sheer wild joy of it knew no bounds.

I got my first dog in the summer of 1917 as a result of a septic foot. I had been paddling in the beck outside our house in search of stickle-backs and red-breasts but I had broken my mother's firm rule that I must always wear old sandshoes in the water. It was the rather disgusting habit of all the people who lived near the beck to throw all their old tins and bottles into it. Perhaps it was not as bad as it sounds in these environment-conscious days because the great brown floods of both summer and winter scoured it clear, and flushed all the debris away into the depths of the Eden at the point where we boys believed the Eden to be of unfathomable depth.

Anyhow, on a bright summer morning at the age of four, when paddling unshod, I stood on a broken bottle and gashed my foot which a week later turned septic, a not infrequent occurrence in the days before antibiotics. And a septic cut had to be taken very seriously in case it caused 'blood-poisoning' which could mean death within a few days. Jimmie Longstaff, the owner of the sawmill died within a week of scratching his hand at work.

I recovered, of course, but I had a huge, fat bandage around my foot for some weeks as well as a number of visits from Dr Sprott which made me very important among my friends. During this period my mother used to sit me outside the front door where everyone who passed had a sympathetic word, though, if truth were told, I was rather enjoying it all. The inconvenience of not being able to run and play was more than compensated for by all the attention I received.

Among my frequent visitors was Jack Withers, the landlord at the Joiners' Arms along the street. One morning he stopped his cart and shouted 'A've got a present for thee, Teddy'. We always used 'thee' and 'thou'. He disappeared into the house, had a word with my mother, then came out and lifted me up into his smelly cart – he was also the village carter and midden-emptier for there was no council refuse collection then. He took me along to the barn behind the pub and showed me his terrier bitch with four pups.

I was completely enraptured by the tiny, brown, bright-eyed creatures which waddled squeaking like mice towards me. I think at that moment I became hopelessly, passionately, and indeed, inordinately fond of dogs – dogs of any breed, shape, colour or size – the look of them, the feel of them, the sound of them, even the doggy smell of them.

I chose one, the perkiest of the lot and he was to be mine as soon as they were weaned in a few weeks. I expected great trouble in persuading my mother to allow me to keep him, especially as we already had a rather disagreeable ginger tom-cat who repulsed all our efforts to establish any decent, friendly relationship with him, but Jack had talked her round and I was delighted to find she immediately agreed. I lived for and dreamt of my puppy; I could think of nothing else.

In the months that followed I suspect that my mother often regretted her decision as she had to run around the house endlessly with a floor cloth. But with every week that passed, bright-eyed little Peter, for I had called him after the Rushbearing day, wheedled his way further and further into the affections of all of us.

He was a small, smooth-haired, fox-brown terrier, a mongrel – probably a cross between a Border or Lakeland terrier and a fox terrier. He had a mercurial personality passing in seconds from ecstasy to dejection. He had more than his share of intelligence and could often anticipate what I was going to say, not merely react to what I was saying or doing, which was remarkable as I myself had all the unpredictability of a very young child. But in terms of the times-seven method of equating the length of a dog's life with a human being's we were about of an age.

There was one troublesome problem with Peter. Some dogs are stay-at-home, others born wanderers and Peter was an inveterate wanderer – quite incurably so. Given the slightest chance he was off over the hills and far away, usually rabbiting, which he did with uncommon skill. But in a deep rural area there is the constant fear of sheep worrying. Even the sanest, best trained dogs can be led astray by others and create horrifying carnage in no time at all especially at lambing time. Dogs, like all mammals, including humans, change character in the group. And there was another danger for a rabbiter like Peter, the dreaded gin trap, that hideous instrument of torture which was still used as one of the two regular methods of catching rabbits, the other being the snare. The trap was set in the entrance to the burrow and lightly covered with soil. As Warcop had a full-time rabbit catcher, straying dogs and cats were constantly being killed or maimed, sometimes tearing off a leg in their terrified frenzy to get free and crawling away to die in agony.

Whenever Peter disappeared my mother organized an immediate search, day or night, until he was found and for me this often meant hours of searching in all his known haunts in the village, in farm yards, in copses, along the beck and generally in broadening circles until he was found, more often than not, sniffing around the rabbit holes in a field or wood a mile or two away. There was no peace in the house until he was safely back, for my mother dreaded a farmer's knock on the door to tell her that Peter had killed a lamb and the thought of him being maimed in a trap terrified her – and me. 'I'll knock that dog's head off,' she always said but she was so relieved to see him back that he always got away with a stiff telling-off.

Peter had another characteristic which was finally to prove his undoing. He formed a number of permanent and violent antipathies to certain of the other village dogs, irrespective of their size, and he was utterly fearless in showing them. His greatest hatred was for an enormous sheepdog called Major, owned by old Tom Grisedale the local farmer with the wrestling sons. Major was more like a wolf than a dog both in appearance and character. He probably had Alsatian blood in him and had been reared purely as a working dog, without affection. He was the most unfriendly, indeed vicious, dog in the village and the detestation between him and Peter was mutual and unrelenting.

Unfortunately Grisedale's cows passed our house four times a day in summer on their way from the field to be milked and each time the wolf dog was there snapping at their heels, strutting evil-eyed along the road as though he owned the place. Whenever he got the chance, Peter, less than half Major's size, was after him, circling around, hair erect, nose down, looking for an opening to attack.

This hatred between the two dogs was known to everyone in the village and anyone within reach kept them apart. But one June day, almost on Peter's fourth birthday, there was no one about except Tom Grisedale who was too slow on his feet to reach them. Perhaps he wanted our dog taught a lesson. Peter flew at the monster like an arrow, grabbing him by the rear leg – his fatal, tactical error for all Major had to do was to turn his head, seize Peter by the neck and shake him like a rat. When I appeared on the scene a few seconds later he threw Peter in the air and he landed six feet away. My beautiful dog lay torn, bleeding and stunned on the dusty road side. I remember vividly the huge torn flap of skin lying over on the bright yellow silver-weed flowers which grew along the edge of the road. What strange little things become indelibly imprinted on our minds at these moments of high tragedy, and this was one of the most awful moments in my short life.

'That'll larn him,' said Tom Grisedale and walked away, and for those words I hated him to the end of his days with a hatred equal to Peter's for his dog. This was quite illogical for he was in most things a kindly man.

I lifted poor, broken Peter in the upturned palms of my two

hands and, as gently as a boy of eight could, I carried him into the house, his blood dripping on to my bare knees. In spite of all the loving care my mother lavished on him he died the next day while I was home from school for my dinner. I cried and cried as my father gently buried him, wrapped in his old blanket, in the black soil of the garden. I wandered away over the hill called Hubers behind the village to be alone with my unbearable grief. I saw him galloping ahead, stopping every few yards to see if I was coming and sniffing at every rabbit hole. If dogs are immortal, which they surely are, Peter was with me on that sad summer afternoon trying to comfort me as he had always done. I stayed away from school, but neither my mother nor the schoolmaster complained. They understood the bond between a boy and his first dog.

My second dog, given to me by a farmer a few months after Peter's death, was a hilarious, lovable disaster. He was a sheepdog puppy, a large black and white hobbledehoy of a dog. He had never before been in a house and immediately began to nibble cushions, curtains, rugs, slippers, indeed almost everything that was not made of iron. As the weeks passed his appetite became more insatiable and more ambitious. As his teeth and jaws grew stronger, chair-legs became his favourite nibble. After three months this, by now huge dog was literally destroying our home and, my mother would say ten times a day, 'You'll have to get rid of that bloomin' dog.' Easier said than done for he had almost grown to adult doghood without being trained to work and, poor Spot, what farmer would want an untrained and by now virtually untrainable, soft, pampered sheepdog? To make matters more difficult he, like Peter, had won the affection of us all.

But life with this great, loping lovable dog, always full of apologies for his misdemeanours, could not continue. My parents persuaded me that it was cruel to keep him as a pet when his place was in the fields and on the fells rounding up sheep with his brothers and sisters. Had it been possible to consult him he would not have agreed with this view of his future. He was perfectly happy leading a life of pampered leisure.

When the time came we were all sad to see him go but at

least, I consoled myself, he was going to a farm where he would be fed, dog-food of course, and have a warm bed, if only of hay in a stable. Of course he would miss the home comforts and my mother's excellent cooking and he would, somehow, have to learn to work for his living, but this after all was the lot of all sheepdogs.

I often saw him around the village in the early weeks after leaving us. He used to come disconsolately to the door asking to be taken back in a way which made it clear that he was sorry for all the trouble he had caused us. But eventually he and I forgot each other.

I acquired my third dog, a pedigree, smooth-haired fox terrier, as a swap. At about the age of ten or eleven I had a tame jackdaw which my brother Len had rescued from a pack of boys in Richmond. It was an emaciated bird when he brought it to Warcop and gave it to me. I kept it in a large wire-netting-covered cage which I made. As with all our pets Jacko was known to everyone. He, like Mary Alice Gregson's parrot, was part of the community. The only problem was that I could not persuade him to talk. 'He'll have to have his tongue slit,' said Greg Wilkinson, the local amateur vet, a process which was to me too terrible even to think about. Once I had built him up he was an attractive bird with grey collar and irridescent black feathers and he was greatly, indeed inordinately, admired by Captain Jim at the Hall. Strange that the Lord of the Manor's son, a barrister, should covet a small boy's pet jackdaw. But he did, and he frequently dropped hints about how he wished the bird was his, all of which I ignored but not without embarrassment.

In the end he got round me in rather a crafty way. One day he invited me to the Hall to see some puppies in the kennels, for they had real iron-barred kennels behind the house. There was never a word about Jacko of course. The effect on me of a fox-terrier bitch with a litter of puppies was exactly what I believe he calculated it would be for he knew I was mad on dogs. Notwithstanding the tenth commandment which, of course, I knew by heart, I wanted one of those puppies to a degree which would have made Moses turn me out of the tribe. But still no mention of Jacko! He allowed me to fondle them and gloat over them for half an hour. Eventually I went home thinking of nothing but a fox terrier puppy.

About a fortnight later I met him in the village. 'By the way, Short', he said (the gentry always called us by our surnames), 'I was just thinking – if you would like one of those pups I'll swap you for your jackdaw.' Now much as I liked Jacko I didn't have to consider the proposition for more than a few seconds. After all, I persuaded myself, a jackdaw isn't much fun. He (or was it she? I didn't even know that) couldn't play and I wasn't even sure that he knew his own name and he did smell a bit. But a dog – why a dog was almost human!

And so I became the overjoyed owner of a smart, bouncy fox terrier called Grip but lost my jackdaw. Unfortunately as he grew bigger and bolder Grip turned out to be even more of a wanderer than Peter. If I took him with me when I went out to play, he either had to be on his lead or I had to watch him all the time which made playing impossible. If I relaxed my vigilance for half a minute he would quietly disappear. Sometimes I chose not to notice when he sneaked off, but I knew that sooner or later my mother would raise the hue and cry until he was found. When I was keeping my eye on him and he started to creep away, he would usually return to heel but with tail down and at his slowest pace, stopping every few yards to sniff at something or other. If however he was more than about fifty yards away he had the infuriating habit of completely ignoring me, indeed of deliberately looking the other way even though I was shouting my head off. What a dog cannot see does not exist for him, so he could be quite alone by the simple expedient of turning his head away.

He was a tough little dog both physically and in his personality. He caught many a rat in Ellwood's stack-yard at Row End farm and occasionally, on one of his expeditions, killed a rabbit which was almost as big as himself. But he was always defeated by the sharp little water rats with which the banks of the beck teemed, all they had to do was to plop into the water and swim away under the surface. Although he would stand on the bank or up to his tummy in the water, he could never see them and was clearly mystified at their disappearance. He looked at the water but, apparently, never into it. Some village dogs were highly successful with the water rats but my Grip, for all his farmyard skill, was hopeless.

Perhaps because of his independent spirit and his toughness I never felt as close to Grip as I had done to Peter. Perhaps it was too early for any dog to replace my first love. He was never 'my' dog in the sense that Peter had been. This is not to say that we had no affection for him, we had, and were proud to own such a smart little dog. After all he was gentry, and in Warcop that set him apart! Perhaps his independence was nothing more than not letting his side down. How little we know about what goes on behind the shining eyes of a dog – probably a good deal more than most of us suspect.

We had Grip for a few years before his wandering was the death of him, as my mother always said it would be. This was not because of sheep-worrying, though we often suspected, but were never quite sure, that he sometimes had fun and games with some of the flocks. Nor was it a gin trap. It was because of the new and growing third menace to wandering dogs in the valley, the motors which by the mid-twenties were passing along the main road every day. There were even two or three in the village by this time. After Donald Wood, our artist, got his solid-tyred Trojan, Sir Arthur Wynne bought a two-seater with a hood and a dickey seat. He was closely followed by the vicar, then a local farmer who lived on a hill farm under the fells bought a splendid shining saloon, used mainly for going to chapel. The Chamleys and Wilds could not be outdone by a hill farmer and soon appeared in new cars. All these dangerous machines travelling along the narrow roads at the speed of trains were a new hazard for dogs – and children.

One evening when he was 'off' we had a message to say that Grip had been knocked down by a car on the main road and that he was lying injured in the grass on the road side. I went on my bicycle to bring him home. I carried him as best I could but the movement must have exacerbated his injuries for he was obviously in great pain and unable to walk.

He died later in the evening and was buried in the garden beside Peter. I mourned for him, but not with the pain I felt when Peter died, partly because he was never so close but also because, sad to relate, I was by now inured to the death of my pets. I always had pets, guinea-pigs, also a gift from the Hall, mice, rabbits, birds – including a young owl – a hedgehog and fish by the score. With this volume of livestock I had to run a veritable undertaking business.

My other dogs lie outside my early childhood but there have only been three others, all living to a ripe old age and, indeed, spanning the half century from my mid-teens to my retirement from Parliament.

My years with Peter, Spot and Grip, especially the four years with Peter must have built something into my character which would not otherwise have been there. The affection that flowed between us could not fail to leave a permanent mark. Could it be that the love and respect I had for them, lesser and more vulnerable creatures, transferred in later life to my feelings about the deprived members of society, also vulnerable and deserving of respect? Too often we forget the part played by animals in the growth of character, personality and beliefs. We acknowledge the influence of heredity, of people, of environment but rarely do we recognize the potency and the value of a close animal-child relationship. It is a startling thought that an important strand in one's political philosophy could be born of a relationship with animals. The dogs I have known and loved from my childhood onwards are part of me today and, dare I say it, a good and wholesome part.

Ten

WHEN I REACHED THE AGE of ten in the week before Christmas, 1922, I was entirely what Warcop had made me, for I had met few people from outside it and never travelled further from it than the day trips to Blackpool and Whitley Bay or my holidays with my Uncle and Aunt in Carlisle. The village was to me a little, secure world into which I had been born and which had protected and taught me ever since. Its values were my values; I was proud to speak its language – both dialect and accent; its people were my people; no door was closed to me – except the gentry's which were closed to everybody except themselves.

And what kind of boy had I become as I reached the threshold from boyhood to youth? Well, I was tall and well-built for my age. This was put down by the school doctor to my mother's famous rice puddings. I was, I am told, a rather serious boy and painfully shy but with a distinctly artistic bent.

Throughout my first decade I had been bombarded by home and school, church and chapel, scouts and Band of Hope with an incessant stream of do's and don't's – buttressed by the carrot and stick of virtue and guilt, sometimes by reward and sometimes by physical punishment. As a result, I had implanted in me a clear, unambiguous code of what was 'right' and what was 'wrong' (according to my mentors!). Faced with alternative courses of behaviour, I did not have to think, all I had to do was refer to the code – my ready-reckoner of morality. Course A was 'right' – follow it and feel good or, better still, be rewarded; Course B was 'wrong' – follow it and feel guilty or be punished. It was as automatic as the tables I had learnt at school. There was no autonomy about my sense of right and wrong at ten, no pondering over the pros and cons of course A as opposed to course B; it was entirely external, code-based and it catered for most of the eventualities of village life. However, if a situation cropped up about which a rule had not been promulgated by my mother or Cranmer or any of my other lawgivers there was always Moses. The ten commandments were a kind of safety net to establish the sinfulness of any doubtful action which might otherwise escape. And adultery had been extended, after the fashion of the rabbinical scholars, to include any uncleanness including not only conversation but also knees and necks.

It was not until some years later, in my middle teens, that I began to resent the conditioning I had undergone in those early years. I saw that so often I had been subjected to the miseries of feeling guilty for infringing some rule or other which clearly was no more than a convenience invented by my elders to protect themselves or one of their institutions. Sometimes I had been made to suffer for no more than defying a popular consensus. I then realized that many of the 'sins' which, I had been led to believe, pointed the way to hell were nothing of the sort, that they were not an offence against the great cosmic pattern which regulated all our affairs and which was inherently good but were no more than minor breeches of man-made rules of which, very often I suspected, the Almighty Himself could not approve. That realization was quite a comfort, though the guilt remained and still remains. What is done to us in the first decade can never really be eradicated.

But at ten everything was black or white, good or bad, true or false. I had no doubts – I just knew 'right' from 'wrong'.

Old Mrs Chamley told my mother she saw me as a future Vicar of Warcop. How wrong she was! Contrary to her view of me, I remember revelling in some of the less gentle local pastimes – 'Tally-ho' across the village on early evenings in winter, wrestling in summer, strenuous wandering on the fells, even swarming up the tall scots firs after crows' eggs. True, I was very much attracted by the church and all its ritual, by the quiet places, by my books, but I was equally attracted by the more earthy pleasures of rural life. Perhaps there were two of me, a rather goody-goody boy, but also a more robust, even rather primitive one. The angel and the ape – and what satisfied the one upset the other. But that is the human dilemma. Perhaps I had it more than most.

I was very afraid of girls, though at the age of five I went steady with one for some months. Her name was Janet, the daughter of the gardener at Eden Gate. I used to call for her on my way to school though it took me out of my way. One day I announced at home that I was going to marry her when I grew up. 'Perhaps she won't have you,' said my mother – she always threw cold water on my exuberances. 'Oh yes she will', I replied, 'I've asked her.' I do not think that this can have been strictly true for I have now no recollection whatever of my proposal to Janet.

Needless to say my fear of girls disappeared completely when puberty hit me two or three years later. May Wilkinson's passion for nature study as well as living in an agricultural village with farm animals performing on every side inevitably meant that I knew the facts of life at a quite early age and thought nothing of it. Procreation and birth were everyday, run-of-the-mill parts of the mechanism of the world of nature. Nevertheless it came as something of a shock when another boy told me that babies were produced by the same process. But at ten there was no self-consciousness about it and I accepted this also as a purely mechanical process. How much better than the self-conscious, mid-teen sex education of today.

The village school had left its mark on me. I had undergone, with some pain, an ineradicable grounding in the four Rs (I repeat, in Warcop religion ranked with the other three). I read enthusiastically and quickly but without discrimination, devouring any book I could lay my hands on. I had even read my first Sexton Blakes – unknown to my mother who had banned them from the house. On light evenings I would push the thin paperbacks under my pillow until my mother went downstairs. I then read until the adventures of the intrepid detective and his assistant, Tinker, made my hair stand on end.

Potty Daisy Crosby, portly Walter Wilson, thank you,

wherever you are, for all the wondrous tales you made available to me from your bookcases.

I had another stimulating source of reading material, thanks to the W.I. As well as organizing the weekly distribution of fish they had a magazine club. Each member bought a magazine and, after reading it, passed it on to the next member on a list stuck in the front. She, in turn, kept it for a few days and again passed it on. In this way we had a constant flow of periodicals at home which we could not possibly have afforded ourselves. They even included such upstage journals as *The Review of Reviews* and *The English Review* which I thought pretty dull – anyhow they had no pictures. The *Strand Magazine* was much more to my liking.

Strangely, in spite of all I read, I had difficulty, and still have difficulty, with spelling. My mother, a voracious reader, had the same problem. Maybe a hereditary faculty is involved in spelling. But I have always got by simply by forming the first and last letters clearly and putting a wiggle between.

I knew some grammar and could parse a sentence reasonably accurately. I was fascinated by words, the variety of them, the arrangement of them and their interaction on each other. But I was a frightful show-off in the way I used the longest ones I could find in my compositions (we never used the word 'essay').

Numeracy (I still like those long words!) was never my strong point but I knew my tables like the back of my hand including those with such lovely names as the 'Aliquot parts of a £' and 'Avoirdupois'. They were all in a neat little table book which was a mine of information. I loved the metric system and had indelibly engraved on my memory a chant which went: 'milli, centi, deci, UNIT (loud) Deca, Hecto, Kilo,' indeed I was so convinced of its beautiful simplicity and superiority over rods, poles, perches, grammes, ounces, pounds, gills, pints, quarts, gallons etc., that half a century later, I played an active part in persuading a reluctant Cabinet to adopt the metrication of our currency, weights and measures. Perhaps the metric chant I learnt in Warcop School was the straw that tipped the balance and turned Britain metric! There was one mystery in the tables which I have never fathomed to this day – the evolution of pints, quarts and gallons to hundredweights and tons in something called the 'Dry or Corn Measure' (what things we had to learn!) – but how on earth do pints end up in tons?

In arithmetic I could perform like a circus dog, a whole variety of complicated tricks known as *The Four Rules* with simple numbers, vulgar fractions (I never knew why they were called 'vulgar') and decimals. I knew about percentages and could calculate simple interest and compound interest which was all, to say the least, rather unreal to me. Still, I suppose somebody, somewhere had £28,500 to invest for 7 years at 4½% compound interest – maybe Mrs Wild or Mrs Chamley.

Most of the history and geography lessons developed into gripping stories told by the schoolmaster of his adventures in the war in Europe and Arabia. He had accumulated a great number of garishly coloured picture postcards wherever he went and these stimulated my imagination about far off lands, as did some of the tales I heard from the returned soldiers outside school. But I did learn some elementary history and geography as well.

My historical knowledge reached its peak with the Tudors. Those five Tudor monarchs were such nice tidy, self-contained packages of knowledge and all different. Before them my knowledge grew progressively less and petered out with the Norman Conquest, apart from a faintly discernible island of light a thousand years earlier around Julius Caesar. After them it faded rather sooner, in fact about the time of the 'Glorious Revolution' (why 'glorious'?), and ran into the ground in the morass of the awful Georges. At ten all the kings were 'good' or 'bad' apart from one or two who had special adjectives of their own e.g. Henry VIII was 'bluff' and Mary was 'bloody'.

A curious thing about my knowledge of history is the way in which great events and people are linked in my mind with places in Warcop. I never think of Henry VIII without remembering a certain hedge on Castle Hill or of Richard I without seeing Warcop Tower and the old worn arms of Warcop high up on a farm wall, or of Agincourt without thinking about the flat meadows between the school and the village. The wandering mind of a schoolboy forms strange associations which have little or no logic in them but arise simply because two things happened to come into the mind together.

Geography was mainly a matter of acquiring facts about the British Isles – counties, county towns, industries, rivers, mountains etc. And again there were the interminable chants – 'Ness, Spey, Don, Dee, Tay, Forth' etc., and all of them strangely unrelated to anything I had experienced. It came as a surprise to me some years later to realize that the mysterious 'Pennines' I had learnt in the mountains of England were none other than our own friendly old fells – up to this point they had been as remote as the Apennines – and that the range called the 'Cumbrian Group' was in fact the Lake District which we could see like a distant sierra over the valley to the west. The difference between 'Cumbrian' and 'Cambrian' always foxed me until I discovered that 'Cumbrian' meant it was in Cumberland.

The schoolmaster was a great believer in LOYALTY and THE BRITISH EMPIRE and talked endlessly about both, 'the Mother Country and her children', he called it and I thought of our clocker and its young ducks. We had to learn the names of the Empire children and be able to point them out on the map and explain why the sun never set on them. The map was always Mercator's projection which, of course, made the red parts, especially countries such as Canada, Australia, New Zealand and South Africa which are some distance from the equator, look a good deal bigger than they are. In reality the lines of longitude converge on the two poles but on Mercator's maps they all run parallel from top to bottom.

He also tried to stimulate our somewhat lethargic British pride by breathtaking descriptions of such magnificent events as the Great Coronation Durbar of 1911 for which George V apparently wore a specially made crown which cost the Indian government £60,000 – evidence, if any were needed, of their loyalty to the King Emperor – and projects like the Cape to Cairo (all red) railway which the acquisition of a few ex-German colonies had apparently made possible. This part of our geography was ritualized on Empire Day, 24th May, which we celebrated with song, drama, exhibitions, in fact anything that would help us to swell with pride at the glories of the British

Empire and the achievements of its peoples. We were all agreed, however, that a half day's holiday would have made us much more kindly disposed towards the Empire.

In the daily scripture lesson I had memorized the Church Catechism by the age of ten including the more obscure bits on the sacraments towards the end and of course the ten commandments but I never understood why, when asked my name, I had to reply 'N or M' when everybody knew I was called Teddy Short. I was also puzzled by the question: 'What did thy Godfather and Godmother then for thee?' Was 'then' a strange verb which I did not know, some peculiar service or rite my godparents had performed for me? But I was much too shy to run the risk of appearing to be silly by asking.

I knew the seasons of the church's year including that funny trio of Sundays which come before Lent known as Septuagesima, Sexagesima and Quinquagesima which I always visualized as three rather old, quaintly-dressed women. And I could name the colours associated with each season. All these were a hangover from the days of universal illiteracy but in Warcop School they still had to be learnt.

The Collects, many of which I had to memorize were pleasanter, self-contained and therefore easier to learn than the rather arid theology of the catechism. Some of them became so much a part of me that when Tony Benn was trying to persuade the Cabinet to continue to support Concord (it had no 'e' then) the words: 'Lover of concord', from the second collect for peace at matins came into my mind and ever afterwards I have thought of Tony as the lover of concord.

Though I loathed learning it at the time, I am glad now that I had to learn by heart so much memorable prose from the Book of Common Prayer which surely represents the high water mark of the English language. I can think of no more beautiful or economical language than that, for example, in the collect to which I have just referred nor any which expresses better that central theme of the Christian ethic, the reconciling of service and freedom '. . . whose service is perfect freedom.'

There was one aspect of our village schooling which went far beyond the learning of facts or the memorizing of religious passages, thanks to the second teacher in the Big Room – May

Wilkinson, the sister of Greg — farmer, amateur vet, local historian, auctioneer. She was passionately fond of the countryside, though it should never be assumed that all village people were, or are. Some who had lived all their lives in Warcop regarded nature as an enemy to be subjugated and kept in its place; others hated it. But May Wilkinson was incurably inquisitive about everything in nature, the teeming life of the soil, the hedges, the woods, the fields, the beck — and her enthusiasm was of that rare kind which is contagious. I caught it, not from her overt teaching but as if touched by the flame of her enthusiasm.

Apart from the necessary time honoured and well-understood offerings which were proffered from time to time to turn away her wrath about something done which ought not to have been done, or not done which ought to have been done (Cranmer still finds his echo in me!), she received from her pupils a never-ending flow of material gleaned from the countryside. Her large square table was permanently cluttered with such things as birds' (sometimes rabbits' or sheep's) skulls, boxes containing beetles, fossils, fungi opening buds or autumn leaves and pot jam jars filled with named wild flowers. On the wide window sills she had an aquarium (a large accumulator jar begged from the sawmill) which teemed with sticklebacks, caddis larvae, water snails, etc, and a vivarium devoted mainly to earth worms, wireworms, centipedes, millipedes, and other secret creatures that live in the soil. In spring there were jars of frog and toad spawn all over the place in varying stages of incubation, and all the year round there seemed to be peas and beans germinating between the walls of sphagnum-filled glass jam jars and the pink blotting paper with which they were lined. It was a great wonder and mystery to me that no matter how we twiddled them, and she always encouraged us to do so, the plumule always grew up and the root down. I couldn't fox those two organs about their identity. The sun and gravity were clearly omnipotent and would have their way.

Her invariable advice about every specimen we brought her was to draw it — draw everything — in our nature books with their pages of drawing paper interleaved with lined sheets. How wise this advice was. My drawing of a strange beetle which I had found on the way to school may not have been a work of art nor scientifically accurate but the drawing of it did ensure that I knew how many legs it had, the shape of its head, thorax and abdomen, the size of its antennae etc. The simple rule 'draw it' created in me the habit of observing the small things in nature and they are so much more interesting than the big things. Shortly after I had graduated from the Infants' Room to the first of her classes, standard 2 in the Big Room, my mother met her one day and asked how I was getting on at school. 'Oh – he's marvellous at finding spiders' nests,' May replied. This shocked my mother whose views on what education should be about stopped far short of spiders' nests.

But May Wilkinson taught me more than observation. She gave me a life-long interest in nature – in the great, inter-locking pattern of life around us. Of course at ten I knew nothing of any universal pattern, interlocking or otherwise – I simply enjoyed and absorbed her enthusiasm. And as with the memorizing of great wodges of the Book of Common Prayer and the Authorized Version of the Bible, it all fell into place years later and became a coherent part of my adult view of life. May Wilkinson, unqualified but unequalled teacher, kindled something in me which has never been extinguished. She gave me that insatiable curiosity about the great reservoir of life on our planet, which has often proved a source of joy when other sources have failed me.

Although, at ten, I seemed to have learnt a prodigious amount in my five years at school, what I had acquired there, apart from my love of nature, was really nothing more than a few useful skills with words and numbers, a collection of facts which were not blindingly relevant to my life in Warcop and a memorized anthology of theological prose – most of which I did not understand. The other ninety-five per cent of my education up to that time had come from the village community which had always passed on to each new generation – and indeed felt obliged to do so – its knowledge, its crafts, its hobbies and its lore. This was community education in its original sense, and how rich and varied it was! The establish-ment of the village schools in the nineteenth century by the two national societies and, after 1870, by the new School

Boards scarcely dented the old communal sense of responsibility for seeing that the next generation were brought up as useful members of the community. Thinking about this in adult life I believe that the communal sense of responsibility was often stronger than the individual family sense of responsibility, though, of course, some parents (including my own) were passionately keen that their children should 'get on'. But they, like the rest, were also keen that *all* the children in the village should become accomplished in *all* the skills and graces of rural living. So I got what early education I had beyond the four Rs from our own village people. Willie Savage of the Band of Hope taught me much, rather by example than precept, and my close association with the vicar gave me even more. Miss Hill the scoutmaster taught me what she believed were the manly virtues as set out in 'Scouting for Boys' as well as many handicrafts besides. From Jack Withers I learnt about dogs, from Jack Walker at the Railway Inn how to fish; from Captain Tim about birds. Ned Burrow the deaf cobbler gave me a love of poetry and Donald Wood did the same for me with drawing and painting. Jimmie Gardiner taught me to make wireless sets and from Willie Watt I developed skill and standards in gardening. I learnt woodwork in the joiners' shop at the sawmill and metalwork at the smithy. Captain Jim made me play a straight bat and keep my eye on the ball – rules which have wider application than cricket. What a marvellous education Warcop was!

Rural children had to get their wider education where they could, but I was fortunate for in our village the opportunities were there if our parents allowed us to profit by them – as mine did. Unfortunately some put most of the really educational places such as the smithy or sawmill out of bounds to their children and, in so doing, deprived them of the sort of creative opportunities which are simulated today in the schools.

Girls were taught at a quite early age all the domestic skills which their mothers considered necessary. They learnt to cook and bake; to scrub, poss and mangle the clothes; to polish furniture and wash floors; to knit, sew, darn, crochet, embroider and make hearth-rugs; to make jam, marmalade and wine. It was all part of the continuity of village life.

No one knows at the time when a new era is beginning. Day succeeds day, each one only imperceptibly, if at all, different from the one before. Events occur which may or may not be significant. There is no way of knowing until long afterwards. Only time can give them significance and can show up in high relief the beginnings of a new era. Looking back now, my first five years at school, from 1918 to 1922, were indeed the start of a new age though few at the time would have believed it had they been told it was so.

Looking back, it now seems obvious that the old sense of responsibility of the village for the communal education of its children was just beginning to be eroded by higher wages after the war, by cheaper transport and the freedom to shop further afield, by mass-production under the impetus of war and the consequent influx of cheaper consumer goods into the shops in the market towns.

Why slave away making a hearth-rug when cheap and durable rugs were on sale in Penrith? Why bother to make jam or marmalade or bake bread when the Co-op would deliver them from their shop in Appleby? And, sadly, the change was not merely a matter of convenience, for many people were beginning to *prefer* the often shoddy, mass-produced articles to those produced in sturdy but cruder form in the village. They represented what was believed to be a smarter, more up-to-date world outside the village. As the twenties progressed everybody pursued modernity but often at the cost of traditional values and quality. There was, probably for the first time, an incipient dissatisfaction with village life which may well have been fuelled by the fifty-three soldiers who returned from the war feeling unsettled and uncertain about the future. The tempo of life everywhere was quickening. The internal combustion engine and wireless were breaking down the immunity of small remote communities such as ours to changes outside.

Wartime levels of taxation and the social reforms of Lloyd George were reducing the peaks and the hollows in the distribution of wealth though these were still colossal. In Warcop the gentry, though still rich by our standards, were poorer and had fewer servants after the war but the farmers were better off and, on the whole had done well out of the war.

The Labour Party, pledged then as now to a radical redistribution of wealth, was gathering strength and won 147 seats at the General Election in 1922, my tenth year. Fifteen months later the first Labour Government was formed.

But in spite of the changes we were still a poor community – at least as far as material possessions were concerned, though given our idyllic environment and the fact that, apart from the gentry, we were all more or less in the same boat, our poverty did not show. Not only did it not show but we did not know we were deprived. The consciousness of deprivation came later as the barriers between the valley and the outside world were broken down.

There were few modern amenities in the village. Travel was then – as now – a special problem. In 1922 the number of motors could be counted on one hand and a regular bus service to the market towns had not yet started, though there were about four local trains a day in each direction. Unfortunately the nineteenth century landowners had made sure that the station was sited a long way from the village and this made the trains very inconvenient. Most of us had home-made bicycles; there was a constant swapping of wheels, axles, frames, handlebars, etc and the resultant creations ranged from tyreless boneshakers to sleek-looking machines, which seemed almost new. A few of the older boys in their late teens managed to get motor bikes and, later in the twenties, one very daring young lady, my sister, acquired an A.J.S. 2¾ h.p. machine.

There were no private telephones and, I believe, only three wireless sets.

Hardly anyone had hot water or indoor sanitation. No one had a vacuum cleaner though the Ewbank carpet sweeper was catching on. Few houses had electric light and no one cooked with electricity or bottled gas, but the new Valor oil stove with a portable oven on top had made its appearance. The coal-fired kitchen range was universal. Imagine having to light the fire before the kettle could be boiled for breakfast!

Looking back now it is obvious that the signs of change were there but so far they had made little impact on our everyday lives. In fact I believe some people in Warcop in 1922, including my father, were looking backward, rather than forward to a brave new world. They wanted a return to the 'good old days' they said they had known in that magical era about which I heard so much – 'before the war'. Too often I suspect they were really yearning for their own lost youth as men have always done.

They did not know, they could not know, that their 'before the war' world had gone forever. The age of motor cars, wireless, saxophones, short skirts, the Charleston, the General Strike, the Great Depression and Hitler was dawning.

Eight days before Christmas 1922 I entered my second decade but, without knowing it, I also entered a different world. I loved my home, I loved my village and felt a part of it. I hoped it would go on as it had done and that I would be there for ever. But soon my path was to take me over the hills and far away to a different world of which I knew nothing.